Understanding Bipolar Disorder

Understanding
BIPOLAR DISORDER
THE ESSENTIAL FAMILY GUIDE

Tools to Thrive Together

Aimee Daramus, PsyD

callisto
publishing
an imprint of Sourcebooks

Copyright © 2020 by Callisto Publishing LLC
Cover and internal design © 2020 by Callisto Publishing LLC
Author photo courtesy of © Kilroy Dunne Photography
Interior and Cover Designer: Stephanie Sumulong
Art Producer: Hannah Dickerson
Editor: Samantha Barbaro
Production Editor: Nora Milman

Published by Callisto Publishing LLC C/O Sourcebooks LLC
P.O. Box 4410, Naperville, Illinois 60567-4410
(630) 961-3900
callistopublishing.com

Printed and bound in China
OGP 2

With thanks to all of the clients and mental health advocates whose stories and lives gave me the knowledge to write this book.

While I've been very fortunate in my mentors, for this book I owe special thanks to my two most important mentors in the area of psychopathology: Dr. Jerry Westermeyer and Dr. Robert T. Baker.

Contents

Introduction and How to Use This Book

This book is a practical guide for people whose family members are among the 2 million-plus Americans living with bipolar disorder. The disorder causes drastic shifts in mood and energy, which can be confusing, frustrating, and overwhelming for the person experiencing them—and for the people supporting them. If your loved one was recently diagnosed with bipolar, you likely have a lot of questions, fears, and concerns about how to help them live the healthiest life possible. This book will try to answer all those questions as well as teach you how to improve communication with your family member and create a support system that works for everyone.

Families are an essential part of bipolar treatment, because they can have such a deep impact on recovery. Studies have shown that supportive family members help people with bipolar disorder become more emotionally stable, stay on top of medications and appointments, and identify mood episodes earlier. Conversely, research shows that unsupportive loved ones and emotional toxicity can be as dangerous to recovery as skipping medication doses. In my 20-plus years working in mental health, I've seen the difference that a supportive family can make. Family members can help with everything from taking medications and getting to appointments, to coping with depressed thinking and finding healthier outlets for the excess energy from mania or hypomania. This book will help you learn how to best support your family member with bipolar disorder, while also managing your and your family's stress levels and preventing emotional burnout.

The book is divided into three sections. Part I covers diagnosis: what bipolar is, how it's diagnosed, and the other disorders that bipolar is often misdiagnosed as. The second part dives into the wide variety of treatments available, including medications, therapies, and community support. Part III includes tools to help you work together as a family and thrive, while also acknowledging the presence of bipolar disorder in a realistic way.

Throughout the book, I draw from clinical studies as well as my own career—I've spent more than 20 years working everywhere from hospital psych units to private practice. In my practice, I've treated hospital patients whose mania caused them to take dangerous risks and to not sleep for days, people who have already fought their way to stability and are enjoying a life of work and healthy relationships, and many people at stages of recovery between these two extremes. I'm speaking from my own professional experience, but also from my clients' expertise on living with bipolar disorder.

Throughout the book, I use the term "bipolar" interchangeably with "bipolar disorder." I also use the term "family" throughout to mean supportive loved ones. This might mean blood relatives or a support system of friends and "chosen family." No matter how you're connected to your loved one with bipolar disorder, I hope that this book will help you understand them better.

PART I

What Is It Like to Have Bipolar Disorder?

In part 1, you'll learn to understand bipolar disorder itself. In chapter 1, you'll explore the real experiences of life with bipolar disorder. Chapter 2 focuses on diagnoses, including who can diagnose, what the process of diagnosis actually entails, and what to do if you disagree with the diagnosis. Chapter 3 addresses the myths and realities of bipolar disorder, current scientific research, and how to steer clear of misinformation about the disorder.

Experiencing Bipolar Disorder

Bipolar is a psychiatric disorder characterized by mood swings called "mood episodes," which can take a person from grandiose thinking and euphoria to lethargy and suicidal ideation. There's no set schedule for how a person with bipolar disorder moves through mood episodes; the length and cause of cycles vary from person to person.

Though there are a few different forms of bipolar disorder, common traits include impulsive behavior, excess energy, and strong emotions that don't always seem to make sense. A person with bipolar disorder doesn't usually have a lot of control over those symptoms at first. Still, it can be difficult to understand and empathize with your family member with bipolar, because their behavior during a mood episode may seem strange, upsetting, or hurtful. In fact, some symptoms may lead a person experiencing a mood episode to react badly to genuine attempts to help.

In this chapter you'll learn about what someone may experience during a mood episode, as well as communication skills to help your family understand one another's needs and experiences of bipolar disorder.

It's Different for Everyone

Sam, a man in his early 20s, had his third serious depressive episode. Therapy did not seem to be working for him, so he tried an antidepressant. However, soon after Sam began taking his medication, he began acting impulsively as he had in his teens. He also had trouble sleeping. Sam gave therapy another try. His therapist noticed how Sam shifted between feeling depressed and feeling impulsive and unable to sleep. He was diagnosed with bipolar disorder, type II.

Dina, a young woman in her late teens, was experiencing periods of depression. During these times, Dina struggled with self-hatred and suicidal thoughts, and slept for many hours each day. These periods alternated with episodes of high energy and insomnia, where she made lots of impulsive decisions, put unrealistic demands on her family, and was compulsively preoccupied with sex. After seeing a therapist and then a psychiatrist, Dina was diagnosed with bipolar disorder.

It Affects Families Differently

Families have different ways of reacting to a loved one's bipolar symptoms or diagnosis. That reaction is usually influenced by factors like their knowledge of mental illness, cultural values about mental health, and accuracy of information.

Sam's family noticed that therapy didn't work for him, and they were relieved at first when he agreed to try an antidepressant instead. But when they noticed his sudden insomnia and impulsive behavior, they were confused. They convinced him to see his therapist again, and felt somewhat relieved when he got his diagnosis—at least now they understood why he had been acting the way he did. But they also felt worried about whether he would still be able to achieve his goal of becoming a college professor.

Dina's family initially attempted to help her with affection, understanding, prayer, and tough love. They were reluctant to take her to see a therapist. While medications and therapy worked, Dina's family still felt guilt that their love for her was not enough. Like many people, they believed that family problems were the main cause of mental illness.

Neither Dina's nor Sam's families were responsible for their bipolar disorder. But that didn't stop their families from feeling guilty that they had caused their disorders, or worried that they let them down by not recognizing their symptoms sooner.

Common reactions to a family member's diagnosis include:

Disbelief or denial. A diagnosis can be difficult to face up to. You might feel the urge to seek out any other possible explanation, or to ignore the situation entirely.

Relief at having an understandable explanation. Your family member's struggles suddenly make sense, and you see a way forward.

Grief and anger. You might feel upset about how this will change your loved one's future, or about the loss of a "normal" life due to changes that must be made to family roles.

Jumping right into action. You're ready to read all the literature and analyze every form of treatment. Though this reaction can be helpful and productive, eventually, you'll have to slow down and let yourself acknowledge your emotions.

Blame. You want this to be someone's fault, because if you can convince yourself that it is, you can also convince yourself that maybe you can make the situation go away (it won't). Blame is an understandable reaction, but it doesn't help.

All these reactions, as harsh as they may seem, are normal and common, though it's not always helpful to act on them. The best way to sort through your feelings is to get better informed about what your family member is experiencing.

Defining Bipolar Disorder

Bipolar is a psychiatric disorder characterized by mood episodes. There are four types of mood episodes—depressed, manic, hypomanic, and mixed. People with bipolar disorder have long periods (weeks or months, maybe more) of depression, which eventually shifts into mania or hypomania: a time of high energy, impulsivity, excessive confidence, and little to no sleep.

Bipolar disorder generally has a genetic or other biological cause, but stress and coping skills can affect the way it appears in daily life.

The Many Forms of Mania

There are two types of manic episodes—mania and hypomania. Family members who don't suffer from bipolar disorder will often feel worried and angry about the irrational behavior of someone in a manic or hypomanic episode. That's because it's hard to understand how little control someone has over themselves during mania.

Mania

Louis arrived at the hospital while he was having a manic episode. He signed some of the paperwork and then felt the need to walk up and down the hall before continuing the admission. He was easily distracted and asked a million questions, some of which had nothing to do with the hospitalization. He tried to pay attention to what the hospital workers were saying to him, but he found it difficult.

The symptoms of mania include high energy despite not sleeping, elevated mood, impulsive behavior, grandiosity, racing thoughts, and difficulty paying attention.

Elevated mood means feeling unusually happy or excited over small things, or even feeling "high" despite not using drugs. Not everyone experiencing a manic episode feels happy, though; they might also feel easily irritated, especially if you try to slow them down or stop them from carrying out a bad idea.

Impulsive behavior can include unusual drinking or drug use, spending money until deeply in debt, unsafe sexual behavior, or creative or artistic binges. Someone having a manic episode may drive recklessly or exercise to the point of serious injury.

Grandiosity is the belief that one has powers or privileges that they do not in reality possess. It can manifest as being very demanding or even clearly delusional. Someone in the midst of a manic episode might expect immediate gratification of demands. They might talk nonstop about new projects that they've never thought about before and expect to be successful immediately. They might even temporarily believe that they're someone powerful, like a CEO or a spiritual leader.

Hypomania

Tim was a successful salesman who occasionally took time off because he had serious depressive episodes. During hypomania, though, he could work all day, leave the office to hang out with friends or go on a date, then finish some paperwork at home. He regularly needed only three to five hours of sleep for weeks at a time.

Hypomania is like mania, but less severe. A person experiencing hypomania will have high energy and be able to feel good on very little sleep. They feel confident but not grandiose. People with hypomania might take on more work than usual, have trouble concentrating, and be irritable, especially if someone is trying to slow them down.

Here are how a few symptoms look different in mania and hypomania.

Energy Level

While someone with mania may not sleep for days and may not even be able to sit down, someone with hypomania will sleep for a few hours (maybe three to five hours instead of eight) and still easily keep up with a demanding schedule.

Confidence and Self-Perception

While in the midst of a hypomanic episode, Imani suddenly decided to become a beauty influencer, even though she had never expressed interest in that career before. She used her credit card to pay for expensive clothes, a website, and a launch party. Once the hypomanic episode ended, she never mentioned these plans again, except to her therapist. She had to budget carefully over the following years to pay off the debt she had run up.

During hypomania, confidence and self-image are higher than normal. That can make a person charming and persuasive. While impulsivity during manic episodes can lead people to take life-threatening risks, risky behavior due to hypomania is generally less dangerous or damaging.

Euphoria

Euphoria is a feeling of unusual happiness, excitement or enthusiasm. During mania, the elevated mood is usually too extreme to be charming. In hypomania, euphoria can feel like a lot of fun, though it definitely contributes to impulsiveness.

Irritability

Irritability usually occurs when others try to get the person experiencing a manic or hypomanic episode to slow down. They might react poorly to attempts to talk them out of something or persuade them to be realistic. Someone experiencing hypomania may be a little easier to persuade and have a less extreme irritable reaction.

What Depression Looks Like

Tanya, a married mother of two in her 40s, had a number of brief periods where she was frequently angry and irritable. During these periods, she also experienced insomnia and overspent so badly that she had to declare bankruptcy twice. Now, though, she was barely able to get out of bed to go to work. She slept more than 12 hours a day when she was able to, experienced crying spells, and had a sad mood, low energy, and no motivation to do anything. She didn't feel any pleasure in the things she normally enjoyed.

The main symptoms of depression are sadness or emotional numbness, excessive sleep and insomnia, fatigue during the day, unexpected changes in appetite, lack of motivation, little to no ability to feel pleasure, self-isolation, and irritability. Not everyone suffering from depression has every symptom, however.

Energy Level

When someone has depression (also called a depressive episode), they typically have low energy. This can range from feeling tired but getting through the day, to a fatigue so deep that it's difficult to get out of bed long enough to eat or take a quick shower. This is a real symptom, and shouldn't be labeled as laziness. Someone who is lazy probably has plenty of energy to do the things they enjoy. Someone whose fatigue is caused by depression won't be able to do a lot of the things they like.

Confidence and Self-Perception

One of the most difficult aspects of depression is what it does to the thoughts and self-image of the person experiencing it. They may genuinely feel that they are unwanted, that they ruin everything they try to do, that they are failures, or that they are unloved. They may also have a lot of guilt about what their disorder is doing to the rest of their family. This change in thinking is a symptom of a disorder.

Suicidal Thoughts

This is a difficult topic for anyone to think about, especially in relation to a loved one. But 25 to 50 percent of people who have bipolar disorder will attempt suicide at some point, most commonly during a depressive episode. If your family member appears to be experiencing a depressive episode, it's important to find the courage to ask them if they have thought about harming themselves. If they say yes, ask if they have a plan and if they intend to attempt it soon. Having a "realistic plan" means that they have chosen a method that is easily accessible to them. If they have a goal of completing the act within a day or two, that's much more serious than if they have a plan but no immediate intent. If they have a realistic plan and are at risk of attempting within the next few hours or days, take them to the emergency room immediately.

If they aren't in immediate danger, make a suicide prevention plan. A suicide prevention plan is a document that lists actions to take when someone begins having suicidal thoughts. It should include calling their psychologist and psychiatrist as soon as the suicidal thoughts start. A family member or two should be designated to keep in daily contact with them while these thoughts persist; one person should be looking after them at every moment and available to take them to the hospital if it becomes an emergency (family members can take turns in this role). The suicide prevention plan also includes knowing which supportive friends and family are willing to talk to them on the phone as well as listing hotlines they can call.

There are hotlines and suicide prevention phone apps listed in the Resource section of this book (page 150). They'll help you make plans for keeping your family member safe and offer suggestions about how to start this difficult discussion.

Mixed Episodes

Bryan, a college student, was feeling many of the thoughts and emotions that people with depression experience, including sadness, guilt over nothing, feeling unwanted and left out, and seeing himself as a failure despite evidence that he was excelling. Yet, he also acted very different from a person in a depressive episode. He had a lot of energy despite only getting three or four hours of sleep a night for weeks. He spent too much money and drank impulsively, assuring his friends and family that it was fine and he felt terrific.

While people with bipolar disorder usually alternate between depression and mania or hypomania, some people have "mixed" episodes. In a mixed episode, there are symptoms of depression as well as manic or hypomanic symptoms. In the previous example, Bryan has depressed thoughts but the energy levels and impulsivity found in hypomania. This can make a mixed episode harder to diagnose, especially if diagnosis is confused with the use of drugs or alcohol.

DO THIS TOGETHER

If your family member has already been diagnosed, it's important to recognize the first signs of a mood shift going forward. Identifying a mood episode early on can lessen its intensity and ensure that your loved one receives correct treatment.

Sit down together and write down the first signs of each mood state that they've experienced. Write down the way it felt to the person experiencing it as well as how it appeared to family members.

The first sign of mania or hypomania is often insomnia or reckless spending, for example, but your family member's may be different. The first sign of a depressed mood could be low self-esteem or daytime sleepiness, but these are just examples. In the future, this list will let you know when a new mood state is coming, so you can tell the treatment team and start preparing.

If your loved one hasn't been diagnosed yet, get together and write down all the signs that might be symptoms of bipolar disorder. What type of mood episode do you think your family member might have had? Did they notice the same thing? What were the first signs that something might be wrong?

Often, the person with bipolar and the family may experience the same symptoms very differently. For example, your family member may neglect chores, work, or homework during a depressive episode because they are experiencing exhaustion, but the family may see it as a discipline issue.

How Often Do Cycles Occur?

A "cycle" is a period of time in which someone with bipolar experiences both depression and mania or hypomania. "Cycling" is the pattern of changes in someone's mood episodes. Cycling can be triggered by a stressful event, but it is not always. Some people have a seasonal cycling pattern—for example, experiencing depression in the winter and spring, then hypomania in the fall. Sometimes there's no immediate explanation for why moods change when they do. Cycling differs a lot between individuals, even those in the same family. But as a person begins to track their cycling, a pattern will usually start to emerge.

In the most typical pattern of cycling, a mood episode cycle lasts weeks or months. For some people with bipolar, the cycle may be only days long, and for others, it may last for years. That makes it hard to diagnose accurately, especially if the first episode of someone's life is a depressive episode. In those cases, it may be a long time before they have a manic or hypomanic episode, and thus a long time before anyone realizes that they are experiencing bipolar disorder.

Moods and Family

Brendan's first mood episode was a manic one. He often worked all night on designing software that he hoped to sell to NASA, despite a lack of formal qualifications or training. On other nights, he went out and walked around the city, talking with strangers. Because the family had no known history of bipolar disorder, they initially assumed that he was using drugs. But testing showed no drug use and only a moderate amount of alcohol. Brendan didn't listen to his parents' concerns about his safety or about his unrealistic hopes for the future and became upset and angry when they tried to talk to him. Once his mood shifted to depression, he suffered intensely. He was skeptical that anything would help, but his emotional pain pushed him to try. His family was able to persuade him to go to the doctor for medication.

When a family member has bipolar disorder, the effect on everyone's lives can be powerful—especially at first, when the disorder isn't particularly well-controlled. Initial diagnosis is an emotional time as roles in the family change. If your family member with bipolar has been living on their own before having a mood episode, it will be hard for them to admit that they can't take care of themselves right now. But they will likely need a lot of help. During a depressive episode, they may not be eating or taking care of basic personal hygiene. They may be at risk of harming themselves. During mania, their impulsivity or irritability could push them into dangerous situations. The patient may need more parenting than they have had in years, which can be hard on everyone, including younger siblings or children who have to make do with less attention from parents than they're used to. Spouses and partners may have to spend more time apart than they like in order to get everything done.

Not all people with bipolar need to move back in with family. For some people, the right medication and therapy plan can let them live on their own for the rest of their lives. Others may need to live with family from time to time when symptoms are severe. A rare few will not be able to function on their own long-term. This varies from person to person and should be decided by figuring out what the current risks are.

High expressed emotion—a psychological metric of how much family members criticize, judge, or talk about the patient—generally predicts a less successful course of treatment. Being shouted at, blamed, or criticized constantly is damaging to anyone, but for someone with bipolar disorder, it can lead to impulsive acting out, or make their low self-worth worse. Even well-meaning family members can be damaging if they act out of their own frustration or need to control the situation.

Emotional overinvolvement is also a part of expressed emotion; constantly hovering over your family member and trying to fix everything can lead to worse outcomes in treatment and burnout in the family members. It's important to respond to symptoms and stay solution-focused. Every family member should learn emotional coping skills to help them manage high-tension situations and have a safe outlet for their own feelings.

One arena to be especially aware of is appointments. Family members may need to take time off from work to bring the person with bipolar to appointments with therapists, psychiatrists, or others. Even if the person has a car or is able to take public transportation, appointments can be nerve-racking at first and emotional support will be crucial. There may also be times when the patient can't or won't go to an appointment without support. People with depression may not have the energy or motivation to go to treatment appointments without help, and people with mania may be too impulsive or overconfident to feel the need to go.

How Much of It Is Personality?

Personality traits are qualities that are a permanent part of who you are. There is often a genetic influence to our personality traits, and life events can influence how strong a trait becomes. Personality traits affect how someone experiences their disorder, how well they cope, the quality of their relationships, and even their likelihood of being overmedicated.

The personality traits most often associated with bipolar disorder are neuroticism, aggressiveness, disinhibition, low openness to experience, low extraversion, and low conscientiousness.

Neuroticism is a state of being easily worried, quick to get upset about things, and slow to relax. People high in neuroticism are often bothered by small details, like temperature, noise levels, or scratchy clothes. They often have strong emotional reactions, and may have less self-control than others. Neuroticism has been connected to several different mental health disorders, including different types of bipolar disorder.

Aggressiveness doesn't necessarily manifest as violence, although it can. It can also mean being quick to confront or anger under stress. When you're in danger and need to take care of yourself, aggression as a personality trait can be a good thing. But when it's unrestrained as a part of bipolar disorder, it can be destructive to relationships.

Disinhibition means that someone is impulsive. As soon as an idea occurs to them, they act on it. They say things without thinking. Being naturally disinhibited could enhance the impulsivity in manic episodes.

Extraversion means someone is energized and copes with stress by being around people and having an active social life. Being low on extraversion means that someone is more introverted and will eventually find that social events drain their energy. People with bipolar disorder often have lower extraversion, which could affect relationships and how they manage depression.

Openness to experience means that you're in touch with your thoughts and feelings, curious, imaginative, and enjoy some variety in your life. Being low on openness to new experience is exactly what it sounds like: You prefer things that are familiar and stable. People with bipolar disorder are often low on openness to experience, which could affect how willing they are to try new treatment options.

Conscientiousness means being hard-working, careful, reliable, and often detailed. People who are high on conscientiousness tend to follow rules. Being low on conscientiousness means that you're not much of a rule follower and may not conform to common beliefs about right and wrong. People with bipolar disorder are often low on conscientiousness, which can lead to careless and disinhibited behavior.

None of these traits directly predict the first episode or the course of the disorder. But they can indirectly affect someone's experience of bipolar disorder, because these traits can make it a lot more difficult to have supportive relationships.

Even the likelihood of being over-medicated is affected by personality. If someone is low on openness to experience, extraversion, and conscientiousness, they have a greater likelihood of being prescribed multiple psychiatric medications. It's not entirely clear why these traits are connected to the use of multiple medications, which is called "polypharmacy." It may be because these traits somehow make bipolar disorder more severe or complex, requiring more medications. It's also possible that these traits make someone less likely to question a doctor's authority, or to push back if a doctor may be overprescribing.

Polypharmacy isn't always a bad thing. Sometimes it's the most evidence-based option. But it also comes with the risk of more side effects and medication interactions, so it's important to understand how your family member interacts with other people, particularly authority figures such as doctors. They may need extra emotional support when raising concerns about medications during appointments, or to get a second opinion if a doctor isn't willing to talk about the patient's concerns.

We've looked at the different types of mood states and how they can affect relationships, how relationships can affect the success of treatment, and the personality traits that are often a part of bipolar. Hopefully, you've started having some discussions about what bipolar has been like so far and written down the first signs and symptoms that your family member shows when a new mood episode is starting. In chapter 2, we'll look at how bipolar is diagnosed, which professionals can diagnose it, and the different diagnoses on the bipolar spectrum.

Decoding the Diagnosis

Now that you have an idea of what bipolar disorder looks and feels like, it's time to dive into diagnosis. In this chapter you'll learn about the process of diagnosis, which professionals can diagnose bipolar disorder, the different types of bipolar disorder, the other disorders that can look a lot like bipolar (but aren't), and some other disorders that are common in people with bipolar.

Getting a Diagnosis

A diagnosis is a shorthand description of a problem. It's not a full description of your loved one's experience, or the family's. Diagnosis does two things for you: It helps your treatment providers identify the right treatments, and it (hopefully) gets your insurance to pay the bill.

But even though it's not the be-all and end-all of treatment, receiving a diagnosis can feel like everything is changing. You may feel like nothing will ever be the same again. Many people also feel relieved when they finally get an explanation for the mysterious problems affecting their family member. Once there's a definition, there are things you can do about it.

Criteria for a Diagnosis

There are several different types of professionals who can diagnose and treat bipolar disorder. The most common are psychologists and psychiatrists. Other health-care professionals may also be able to diagnose and treat bipolar disorder, but their privileges vary by state, country, and insurance, so if you want to see one, you'll need to check who can diagnose, do therapy, or prescribe medication where you live.

A **psychologist** has a doctorate in psychology. In the United States, they also need a state license in order to practice and bill insurance. A psychologist can diagnose and offer therapy. In a few states, psychologists can prescribe psych medications as well.

A **psychiatrist** is an MD. They are legally qualified to diagnose, treat, and prescribe medication. Most psychiatrists don't offer therapy, although they are legally permitted to if they want to. They also haven't received the extensive training in therapy that a psychologist has. A psychiatrist is usually your best option for medication.

Another option for medication is a **psychiatric nurse practitioner**. They have a masters' degree or doctorate in nursing with a specialty in psychiatry. They can prescribe medication, and some also offer therapy.

A **therapist with a master's degree** in psychology, counseling, or social work can offer therapy if they have a state license. A therapist with training and experience in mental illness should be able to diagnose and treat. You may want to check whether your specific insurance limits their privileges.

One thing to be aware of: In many states, the words "therapist" and "counselor" are not protected titles. This means that anybody can legally use those words to describe themselves, open a practice, and treat patients (although they cannot take insurance). It's important to avoid people who have not had appropriate training and thus do not know the correct protocols for treatment, or what to do in an emergency situation, such as when a patient is experiencing suicidal ideation.

To protect people from untrained therapists, every state in the United States has a licensing board. The licensing board issues licenses to therapists who meet the state's specific educational and professional requirements. Licensing boards also list whether a therapist has had a valid complaint against them. To find out whether a therapist you're considering is licensed or has ever had a valid complaint filed against them, you can search online for the name of the state and "licensing board" or "professional regulation."

When you book an appointment with a new therapist, ask about whether they offer a free 15- to 20-minute phone consultation. If someone isn't even willing to take a quick call unless they're getting paid for it, keep looking.

During your free consultation, ask the following questions:

Do you take my insurance?

Do you have training and experience with mental illness?

What services do you provide? (therapy, medication prescription, etc.)

What license do you have?

Make sure to also ask any questions you have about the kind of therapy they offer, what their process is for diagnosing, etc.

It's also fine to look for a therapist of the same gender, race or ethnicity, religion, or sexual orientation as the client. Some people are more comfortable talking to someone with whom they share characteristics like these.

The appointment for diagnosis will take at least a couple of hours. There will be a long series of questions about current and past symptoms, the individual's psychological and medical history, drug and alcohol use, any past trauma, and the family's psychological and medical history. There may be a test of logical thinking and memory called a mental status exam. There may also be multiple-choice or true-false psychological tests that help confirm the diagnosis.

The family member with bipolar will need to sign releases of information before the diagnosing professional can speak with you, and they may also be asked to sign releases for any previous mental health professionals.

A release of information is a form that gives a health-care pro-vider permission to discuss someone's private health-care concerns with others. Due to HIPAA laws, the federal laws protecting private health information, it's illegal for a health-care professional to talk to anyone about a patient—even other doctors—without the patient's written consent, except in certain life-threatening emergencies.

An adult with bipolar disorder has a legal right to refuse to sign a release of information. Because doctors can violate confidentiality in life-threatening emergencies, emergency care can still go forward. However, it is a good idea to have a signed release for at least one family member, so the doctor's office can get the family member's information about symptoms and discuss the meaning of side effects or test results. If a depressive or manic episode prevents the patient from being active in their own care, that release can let a family member help manage the situation.

Types of Bipolar Disorder and Related Mood Disorders

There are a few different disorders on the bipolar spectrum. In fact, it's often called a spectrum because not everyone fits neatly into a specific category.

Bipolar I

→ The person must have had a manic episode lasting for at least a week. They will usually have also experienced depressive and/or hypomanic episodes.

→ Symptoms of the manic episode were severe enough to cause serious impairment in social or professional functioning, or to make hospitalization necessary.

→ During the manic episode, they felt euphoric (cheerful), expansive (larger than life), or irritable.

→ They also experienced one of the three following symptoms (four if the only mood symptom is irritability): grandiosity, decreased need for sleep, feeling more talkative than usual, racing thoughts, easily distractible, increased goal-directed behavior, and excessive involvement in risky activities (impulsivity).

→ The symptoms aren't due to a substance use or to another psychiatric or medical disorder.

Bipolar II

→ The person must have experienced at least one hypomanic episode lasting at least four days, with symptoms present most of the day nearly every day. This must alternate with at least one episode that meets criteria for a depressive episode.

→ They also experienced at least four of the following symptoms during hypomania (enough to see a distinct difference from their usual behavior, but typically not enough to cause a serious problem in functioning): grandiosity, decreased need for sleep, feeling more talkative than usual, racing thoughts, easily distractible, increased goal-directed behavior, and excessive involvement in risky activities (impulsivity).

→ They also experienced at least five of the following symptoms during a depressive episode lasting for a two-week period: depressed mood (irritability if they are a child or adolescent), unexpected weight loss or loss of appetite, insomnia or hypersomnia (excessive sleep), movements that are agitated or unusually slow, low energy or fatigue, feelings of worthlessness or guilt, indecisiveness or difficulty concentrating, lack of interest in pleasurable activities or difficulty feeling pleasure, and significant or recurrent thoughts of suicide or death.

Cyclothymia

→ Cyclothymia is a milder, sometimes faster-cycling form of bipolar disorder. Its symptoms are similar to bipolar II, but they aren't as severe. People with cyclothymia are often misdiagnosed with a depressive disorder, because the hypomanic symptoms present in cyclothymia are so mild that they don't look unusual at first.

→ For at least two years, a person has had symptoms of hypomania that aren't as severe as a hypomanic episode, and symptoms of depression that aren't as severe as a depressive episode.

→ Some people with cyclothymia have hypomanic and depressive symptoms at the same time.

Rapid Cycling

→ Rapid cycling is a "specifier" that can be applied to any type of bipolar disorder, rather than its own diagnosis. A specifier means anything that is different from the usual way that a disorder presents in daily life.

→ Rapid cycling means that a person has experienced four or more distinct mood episodes (depressive, manic, and/or hypomanic) within the same year.

Schizoaffective Disorder, Bipolar Type

→ Schizoaffective disorder, bipolar type, is a diagnosis given when someone has both bipolar I and schizophrenia at once. (There is also a schizoaffective disorder, depressed type, which is not part of the bipolar spectrum.)

→ A person must have experienced at least two of the following symptoms: hallucinations (seeing, hearing, touching, tasting, or smelling things that aren't actually there), delusions (thoughts that aren't real, that are culturally inappropriate for that person, and that that person believes despite evidence), disorganized speech (made-up or nonsensical words, conversations racing from topic to topic), or disorganized or catatonic movements (not moving for long periods of time, sitting in strange positions for a long time).

WHAT DOES "CULTURALLY INAPPROPRIATE" MEAN?

Most of us have cultural beliefs that seem strange or even scary to others, so delusions have to be diagnosed with a knowledge of the patient's culture. For example, if someone believes they are being haunted by a ghost and comes from a family or cultural/religious background where believing in ghosts is normal and harmless, it's not a delusion. Conversely, if nobody in their family or religion believes in ghosts and the person doesn't believe in ghosts when they're stable, it could be a delusion.

Major Depressive Disorder

→   The person must have experienced several of these symptoms: depressed mood (irritability if they are a child or adolescent), unexpected weight loss or loss of appetite, insomnia or hyper-somnia (excessive sleep), movements that are agitated or unusually slow, low energy or fatigue, feelings of worthless-ness or guilt, indecisiveness or difficulty concentrating, lack of interest in pleasurable activities or difficulty feeling plea-sure, and significant or recurrent thoughts of suicide or death.

→   A person with major depressive disorder does not experience periods of mania or hypomania.

MOOD GUIDE

Here's a quick-reference guide to the major moods of bipolar disorder:

Mania. A period of high energy, more impulsive behavior than usual, unusually high self-esteem or grandiosity, and little to no sleep, sometimes with hallucinations or delusions. The mania is severe enough to cause problems in daily life.

Hypomania. A period of high energy, more impulsive behavior than usual, unusually high self-esteem or grandiosity, and little to no sleep. There are few serious problems in daily life and no hallucinations or delusions.

Depression. Sad, numb or irritable, changes in sleep and appetite, doesn't feel much pleasure in anything, and may have thoughts of death or suicide.

Mixed. Symptoms of both depression and either mania or hypomania.

Common Misdiagnoses

There are several reasons why many people with bipolar have difficulty getting a correct diagnosis. One of them is that bipolar disorder can look similar to a number of other disorders, both psychological and medical. Here are the top disorders that bipolar is misdiagnosed as.

Major Depression

Because bipolar disorder includes depressive episodes, it can be mistaken for major depressive disorder. This often happens when the first diagnosis is made during a depressive episode, before a manic or hypomanic episode has occurred. In fact, taking antidepressants will often trigger a person with bipolar's first manic or hypomanic episode.

Anxiety

Bipolar can be misdiagnosed as anxiety because it shares several potential symptoms with manic or hypomanic episodes, including impulsivity and restlessness. But anxiety is an unpleasant experience, while mania and hypomania can feel good. Additionally, anxiety levels will vary according to the immediate situation and can change within the same day, while bipolar cycles change over weeks or months.

Psychosis

If someone has symptoms of psychosis (hallucinations or delusions) as part of a manic episode but shows no other symptoms of schizophrenia, they may be misdiagnosed as having delusional disorder, or schizophrenia or schizoaffective disorder.

Borderline Personality Disorder

Borderline personality disorder is a common misdiagnosis for people with bipolar, as it also involves extreme mood changes, impulsivity, and strong displays of emotion that seem excessive to the situation. The two disorders are also often comorbid, meaning a patient will have both disorders simultaneously. We'll cover this in-depth on page 29. With borderline personality disorder, however, mood changes are sudden, brief, and often stimulated by a feeling of abandonment or rejection. Moods can shift within seconds or minutes, unlike mood episodes in bipolar disorder.

OTHER PERSONALITY DISORDERS

People with bipolar disorder might experience symptoms during a manic or hypomanic episode that could be misdiagnosed as a personality disorder. Common misdiagnoses include narcissism (due to the grandiose thinking and irritable reaction when someone tries to slow them down or tell them they can't do something), histrionic (due to the strong need for attention which may present when more extroverted people enter a manic state) or antisocial (due to impulsiveness and risky behavior).

ADHD

A manic or hypomanic episode can look a lot like attention-deficit/hyperactivity disorder, particularly in children. This misdiagnosis is also common because many people with ADHD become depressed.

It's also possible for these two disorders to be comorbid. In fact, more than 60 percent of people with bipolar disorder have another medical or psychiatric diagnosis as well.

Comorbidity

Comorbidity is when someone has two or more disorders at once. The term can refer to any combination of two or more disorders—two or more medical disorders, two or more psychological disorders, or a combination of medical and psychological disorders. It can be difficult to figure out a comorbid situation, especially when the two disorders share symptoms.

Anxiety

According to one study, 42.7 percent of people who have bipolar will also have an anxiety disorder at some point, such as panic disorder (frequent, unexplained panic attacks), generalized anxiety disorder (anxiety about many different things), social anxiety disorder, phobias, or obsessive-compulsive disorder.

ADHD

There are no reliable statistics on the comorbidity between bipolar disorder and ADHD in children and adolescents. These statistics are complicated because there are three specific types of ADHD (hyperactive type, inattentive type, and combined) and several different types of bipolar disorder. But it is believed to be a fairly common comorbidity.

Both bipolar disorder and ADHD involve high energy, impulsivity, and irritability when others try to slow down the person's plans, so it can be difficult to discern the simultaneous presence of bipolar disorder and ADHD. Euphoria, decreased need for sleep, and racing thoughts are more commonly found in bipolar disorder, and can be a clue that both disorders are present. By late childhood, bedwetting, night terrors, and depression can be a sign that bipolar is present in children. Adults who only have ADHD symptoms will be stable over time, while adults with bipolar disorder will have symptoms that show cycles. Adults who only have ADHD may experience depression but not mania, hypomania, or hallucinations.

Personality Disorders

A personality disorder is when someone's personality traits are taken to such an extreme that their behavior becomes dangerous and self-sabotaging, and they experience difficulty developing and maintaining healthy relationships. Personality is partly genetic and partly due to life experience. You inherit a certain trait, but life experiences such as culture, family, and reactions to that trait can shape how strong it becomes.

When bipolar disorder is comorbid with a personality disorder, coping can be more difficult. Personality disorders are associated with longer mood episodes, shorter periods of feeling happy during mania or hypomania, earlier age of onset, and comorbid substance abuse. In general, the impulsivity of mania or hypomania can exaggerate the symptoms of the personality disorder.

There are 10 personality types/disorders. Because a personality disorder is just a more extreme version of a healthy personality type, you may recognize yourself or your loved one with bipolar in some of these descriptions. But don't worry about it unless it's causing serious problems in work, school, relationships, or another important area of life—those are the signs that traits are true symptoms of a personality disorder.

The ones most commonly comorbid with bipolar disorder are:

Borderline (comorbidity >20%). The symptoms of borderline personality disorder include unstable and unpredictable emotions, unstable relationships, impulsivity, and overly intense, tumultuous relationships with others (over-identifying with others to the point of imitating them, and impulsively rejecting them). Self-harm is common.

Antisocial (comorbidity ~21%). People with antisocial personality disorder can be charming, manipulative, fearless, show little respect for rules or laws, and experience little to no empathy.

Histrionic (comorbidity 5%). Someone with histrionic personality disorder struggles with not being the center of attention. Their words, actions, and style of dress often seem unusually flirtatious to others. They may not care if the attention they get is positive or negative.

Narcissistic (comorbidity 8%). A narcissist needs to feel that they are the best person in the room. An extreme narcissist doesn't feel the need to earn any recognition in order to be treated as such, while a more moderate one will work hard, but feel anger if they aren't given the privilege that they expect.

Substance Abuse

Bipolar disorder is four times as common among people with alcohol use disorder and around five times as common among people with other substance use disorders than it is in the general population. Substance use of any kind predicts a more difficult and less successful course of treatment for bipolar disorder. Intoxication and withdrawal from different drugs can look a lot like the symptoms of a mood episode. Cocaine intoxication, for example, can mimic mania or hypomania; depression is a frequent symptom of cocaine withdrawal.

Drug use can make it difficult or impossible to figure out which symptoms are related to bipolar and which are related to substance abuse. People with alcohol or substance use disorders should have no drugs in their body at the time of their clinical interview for diagnosis.

Trauma

People with bipolar I report trauma more often than people with other types of bipolar. But people with bipolar I and bipolar II experience trauma symptoms in very similar ways. In both, childhood trauma predicts earlier onset of bipolar disorder, more severe mood episodes, and greater likelihood of substance abuse and suicide attempts.

If someone with bipolar has had a trauma in their past, or experiences a trauma during the course of their treatment, treatment providers need to know. That way, they can treat patients for trauma as well and help manage the added risk.

Epilepsy

Epilepsy is present among 3.33 percent of people with bipolar, which is more than twice its rate in the general population. Both illnesses share some features, such as occurring in episodes, rather than having steady and unchanging symptoms. In some forms of epilepsy, seizures can cause temporary changes in mood and behavior or even cause hallucinations and delusions. This is sometimes misdiagnosed as bipolar disorder, schizophrenia, or schizoaffective.

Anticonvulsants (medications used to control seizures) are used to manage bipolar for many patients who do not have epilepsy.

A Note About the DSM-5

The Diagnostic and Statistical Manual of Mental Disorders, 5th edition (*DSM-5*), a book published by the American Psychiatric Association, contains information about every mental disorder acknowledged by modern science. It has the checklist of symptoms for each disorder, detailed information about the main features of the disorder (and other similar disorders), and relevant gender, sexual, and cultural information. The *DSM-5* is used mainly in the United States to diagnose disorders. There have been some concerns about whether the diagnoses presented in the book are influenced by financial or other political concerns.

Outside the United States, mental health diagnosis is done using the *International Classification of Diseases, 10th revision* (*ICD-10*). In the *ICD-10*, bipolar disorder is called "bipolar affective disorder." In both the *DSM-V* and the *ICD-10*, each disorder has a letter-number code for professionals to use on insurance forms and other official paperwork. In the United States, insurance companies generally use *ICD-10* codes. The code F31.0, for example, means "Bipolar Affective Disorder, current episode hypomanic."

Happiness and Quality of Life

Bipolar disorder doesn't mean that your family's chances of happiness are over. There are challenging times ahead, but many people with bipolar disorder have full-time jobs, enjoy satisfying relationships and hobbies, take vacations, and otherwise lead lives that look very similar to those lived by people without bipolar disorder. It's true that some people with bipolar will always need care, but that still doesn't mean a life without work, friendships, or relationships.

While your family is finding the treatment combination that will stabilize moods, you might have to be flexible with your standards and ideas about what constitutes a good life. The better and more thoroughly communicated your treatment is, the more useful the treatment plan will be. This helps everyone have a better quality of life.

DO THIS TOGETHER

Put together a treatment team. The team will need to include at least a prescriber for medication and a therapist experienced with mental illness.

While you're researching:

▸ When you find a professional whom you think might work well, look them up on your state's licensing board website to see if they have a valid license and a clean disciplinary record. Check out their website or social media for more information about them.

▸ Plan out the initial email or call, including any questions you and your loved one have about their experience, education, or approach to treatment.

▸ Check with your insurance to see if the provider and their services are covered.

▸ If there is a choice of providers in your area, think about the options. For example, is your loved one more comfortable with a certain sex/gender, race, religion, or other demographic?

Before the first appointment:

▸ Read the chapters on therapy and medication (pages 69 to 95).

▸ Make sure that your family member has a ride, identification, their insurance information, a debit or credit card for copays, and a list of any questions they still want to ask.

▸ If it will make it easier to remember everything, write out a psychological history and medical history for your family member as well as for their parents and siblings.

> ▶ Be honest with the provider, and urge your family member to do the same. You never know what detail could result in a misdiagnosis or the wrong treatment. Emphasize that you know it will be hard being that honest with a stranger, but it will pay off in better treatment.

After the appointment:

> ▶ Talk about how comfortable your loved one felt with this provider.

What If the Diagnosis Doesn't Feel Accurate?

There are a few reasons a diagnosis may feel wrong. The primary reasons are genuine misdiagnosis and resistance. Resistance is when someone in the family is still resistant to the idea of bipolar disorder or of mental health treatment in general.

If you're worried about misdiagnosis, take a minute to think about the following questions:

→ Do you have specific reasons for doubting the diagnosis? Or is it more of an emotional reaction?

→ How honest was everyone involved with the professional making the diagnosis?

→ Did everyone feel listened to by that provider?

→ Did the provider ignore an important piece of information?

Misdiagnoses happens fairly often, so it's always fair to get a second opinion. Because you'll probably need both a prescriber and a therapist, you already have two opinions. If they agree, it may be a good idea to try their recommendations.

If you're worried about misdiagnosis, write out your reasons for thinking so and how you want to address these concerns. If you're having a strong emotional reaction and you can't understand why, you might be feeling some resistance—especially if your family member has received a second opinion and the two professional opinions agree. Grief and anger are normal parts of diagnosis.

Your feelings are valid. You shouldn't let them interfere with treatment, however. You might need to join an online or in-person support group, begin journaling, spend some time with family or friends to talk about your feelings, or possibly get a therapist of your own. Be assured that, with time and the right psychiatric care, your family can still have good times and good relationships ahead of them.

Now that we've talked about diagnosis, let's talk about what current science says about the causes of bipolar and how it can look different among people of particular sexes, genders, ages, and racial or ethnic groups.

CHAPTER 3

The Science behind Bipolar Disorder

Now that you have an understanding of what bipolar looks like and how it's diagnosed, it's time to take a look at what causes people to develop the disorder. Although bipolar is largely genetic in nature, there are other factors, including gender, that play a role.

We'll also examine the factors that influence the timing of a first mood episode and how stress, substance abuse, trauma, sleep patterns, and relationships can impact the intensity of bipolar symptoms. Finally, we'll discuss the unique needs of children and older adults with bipolar disorder.

What Causes Bipolar Disorder?

Bipolar disorder is linked to a combination of factors, including genetics and other biological vulnerabilities. Though life events don't "cause" anyone to develop bipolar disorder, they can shape how and when bipolar affects someone.

Family and Genetics

Genetic inheritance—having a family member who also has bipolar disorder—is thought to be a primary reason why people develop bipolar disorder. Genetic causes account for between 70 percent and 90 percent of bipolar cases.

But even when someone has a genetic vulnerability to bipolar, developing the disorder is a process—life events change the brain, which eventually leads to a mood episode. Stress and trauma, for example, can change the way that the brain responds to stress. Even one trauma or multiple smaller stressors can cause the parts of the brain that manage fight or flight to treat every small problem like a major emergency, resulting in emotional overreaction to problems that seem minor to everyone else.

People with bipolar disorder may also experience disruption of the reward centers in the brain; these reward centers release chemicals that make us feel "good" in response to certain stimuli. This disruption may influence the lack of pleasure felt in depression or the highs of mania.

People with bipolar also generally experience a disruption of the social and circadian rhythms in the brain, meaning that they have difficulty adjusting to the rhythms of normal daily life, including sleep. Other current research indicates that immune dysfunction, inflammation, and oxidative stress may also influence whether certain people develop bipolar disorder, or how they experience it. However, there is not yet enough information on this theory to draw any definitive conclusions.

Problems during birth may also affect the course of bipolar disorder. People who are born by planned Caesarean section with the use of oxytocin to induce birth have 2.5 times the rate of bipolar disorder than the general population.

Environment

As we discussed in chapter 2, social environments shape the way that bipolar disorder shows up in an individual's life. High expressed emotion in the family, including criticism or judgment from family members, can increase the likelihood of suicidal thoughts and hospitalization. Lower expressed emotion can reduce the severity of mania and depression.

Stress

People with bipolar disorder can be more sensitive to stressful events than people with no mental illness. They also typically report greater life stress right before a mood episode. They may lose sleep or overreact to small stressors. People at the beginning of a depressive episode often withdraw from others or get more irritable, while people heading into a manic or hypomanic state start to sleep less or take bigger risks. It's debatable whether the stress causes the shift in mood or the shift in mood increases sensitivity to stress, and the answer may vary by individual.

Trauma

Early childhood trauma, including emotional neglect, is more common among adults with bipolar disorder than in the general population. People with a history of childhood trauma tend to experience their first mood episode at an earlier age. Childhood trauma can also predict the severity of someone's bipolar disorder as an adult.

Traumatic events in adulthood can affect your family member's experience of bipolar disorder, too. PTSD is a psychological disorder that develops after someone has experienced an intense trauma. Most people who experience PTSD have been sexually assaulted, exposed to dangerous events that risked their life or someone else's, or witnessed any of the aforementioned events. Complex PTSD (C-PTSD) is a type of PTSD that occurs not in reaction to one specific traumatic event, but rather due to ongoing exposure to traumatic events. Someone who experienced childhood abuse or who works as an emergency first responder might experience C-PTSD.

People with bipolar disorder can also be more vulnerable to trauma. This is due to two reasons: mental health stigma and the way that bipolar symptoms can impact decision-making ability.

Mental health stigma means that people are less likely to believe someone with a mental illness if they report abuse or harm. Some predators will target people with mental illnesses because of this. This is another reason why emotional support for people with mental illness can be lifesaving.

Some symptoms can also lead people with bipolar into dangerous situations they'd normally avoid. For example, someone experiencing mania might begin using drugs and alcohol in impulsive ways, become sexually compulsive (hypersexuality), drive recklessly, play dangerous sports without any safety precautions, or go out alone at night—all ways that real people get hurt during mania. These situations can lead to trauma for both the person with bipolar and family members who feel unable to help.

If your family member has PTSD, make sure that their therapist knows, so they can incorporate that knowledge into their treatment.

Drug and Alcohol Abuse

It's common for people with bipolar disorder to develop substance abuse issues. Some people use substances to cope with symptoms, like using alcohol or marijuana to take the edge off a manic episode or blunt the emotions of a depressive episode, or using stimulants to keep going during depression. They might also be coping with the anxiety and stigma that come with knowing that they have a chronic mental illness. Men are more likely to cope using drugs or alcohol than women. The number of manic episodes someone has had, as well as their previous history of suicidal thoughts, are also predictors of developing substance abuse.

The relationship between substance abuse and bipolar disorder is complex. Cannabis use, for example, is associated with an earlier age at the onset of symptoms. This doesn't mean that marijuana causes bipolar disorder, however. It might mean that it could cause it to show up earlier, or that someone was already feeling the mood symptoms and using cannabis to cope before realizing they had bipolar disorder.

For people who had a substance abuse problem before their diagnosis, substance abuse can affect onset, severity, or stimulate a change of mood episode. Substance use may also mask symptoms as well as mimic them, delaying (potentially by years) an accurate diagnosis that would lead to effective treatment.

Sleep

Bipolar disorder disrupts the circadian rhythms that govern sleep. This can lead to delayed sleep or insomnia and influence the severity of depressive episodes as well as the likelihood of suicidal thoughts or attempts.

Sunlight

The amount of sunlight in a particular climate influences the circadian rhythms in the brain. Exposure to more sunlight during childhood can lead to an earlier age of onset, especially in people with a family history of bipolar. That doesn't mean that sunlight causes bipolar. Rather, it means that significant exposure to sunlight can cause onset to happen earlier in life for someone who is already genetically predisposed to the disorder. People living in tropical climates also report fewer depressive episodes.

When Do Symptoms Start?

We've already looked at some factors that influence age of onset, such as trauma, substance use, and even sunlight. Geography has a strong influence as well. Differences in age of onset are found all over the world. For bipolar I, the age of onset in the United States is roughly three to five years earlier than in Europe, although the actual symptoms are the same. The average age of the first mood episode worldwide is 14 to 24, with 15 to 19 being more common in the United States. Cultural differences in risk factors could contribute to this difference. The United States and Brazil tend to be much higher in expressed emotion than many other areas, which may contribute. Bipolar disorder has been diagnosed in children as young as five or six, and around 90 percent of cases are diagnosed by age 50.

Bipolar Disorder in Women

Claire had her first manic episode at age 15. Her grandiosity and impulsivity were seen by her parents and teachers as discipline issues. While many people in her life viewed her as "messed up," she didn't get a diagnosis until after hearing a description of bipolar disorder on a news program as an adult. With medications and therapy, she stabilized, but a planned pregnancy years later resulted in dramatic mood shifts. The pregnancy changed the way her medications worked in her body, and she was unable to fully restabilize until after the postnatal period was over. During menopause, her moods became less stable and she had another round of medication adjustments. As she aged, she found that she had more cognitive decline and required more assistance with daily tasks than other physically healthy people her age. Her doctor referred her for dementia tests every couple of years, recognizing her added risk.

Across sex and gender, people are less likely to seek care for psychological problems than physical problems. But when it comes to bipolar disorder, there are a few symptom differences between the sexes: 75 percent of adults with rapid-cycling bipolar disorder are women, and women have slightly more depressive episodes than men. Thyroid problems are more common in women than in men and more common in people with bipolar disorder than in the general population. Many women with bipolar disorder also report unexplained pelvic pain. Pelvic pain is also more common in women with histories of sexual trauma, which may explain the connection.

One possible reason why women are more likely to experience rapid-cycling bipolar is that women have more depressive episodes, and they are therefore more likely to be prescribed antidepressants. Antidepressants can trigger the shift to a manic episode, which could lead to the start of a faster cycle between depression and mania.

Hormone Fluctuations

Many women report symptom changes based on menstrual cycle, pregnancy, the postpartum period, and perimenopause. It can be difficult to tell hormonal changes from a change in mood episode. If someone is feeling the first signs of a depressive episode but attributes it to perimenopause or PMS, she may not tell her psychiatrist, as women's mood episodes are often dismissed as "hormones." Providers will need to help women identify these patterns and use additional coping skills when necessary.

Pregnancy and Postpartum

Pregnancy and pregnancy loss also affect how symptoms present and how medications work. The prescriber and therapist should be part of the pregnancy team so they can adjust medication and help make life adjustments as emotions, energy levels, and general feelings of wellness fluctuate.

Bipolar in Men

Chris took time off from college to go to inpatient treatment for substance abuse. Among his friends, casual substance use was common. But for him, substances also helped disguise mood swings. During treatment, it became clear that he was actually in the middle of a manic episode that had been disguised by his use of stimulants.

Even with medications, Chris's bipolar disorder was difficult to stabilize—he kept an irregular sleep schedule, and his social life meant he was unable to avoid having drugs and alcohol in his environment. Quitting substances would have meant losing a lot of his college friends. He didn't stabilize until after he graduated and started a full-time job.

Men are less likely than women to be rapid-cycling, and they have fewer depressive episodes. Because it's more culturally acceptable for men to take risks, use alcohol and other drugs to excess, and have symptoms of hypersexuality, it can delay the recognition of a manic or hypomanic episode. For some, stabilizing requires them to give up habits that are shared by many of their friends.

There are also still gender biases in treatment. Even when diagnosed correctly as having bipolar disorder, women are more likely to be treated with medications for anxiety or depression, while men are more likely to receive mood stabilizers such as lithium, the drugs usually used for bipolar disorder. Men are less likely than women to be given electroconvulsive shock therapy and less likely to be offered therapy.

Bipolar Children and Teens

Children are more likely to have rapid-cycling bipolar disorder. They also experience extreme irritability as a symptom more often than adults. As they grow from adolescence into adulthood, they'll usually cycle less rapidly and have a more typical adult pattern of mania, hypomania, or depression.

Medication decisions will be different for children. Some studies have shown that anticonvulsants (seizure medications) are more effective in children than mood stabilizers, the typical bipolar treatment. But that decision should be made on an individual basis by a child psychiatrist. Many psych medications were developed for adult bodies and there is far less research on how they work in children and teenagers.

Diagnosing children can also be difficult because there are a few similar disorders. ADHD, oppositional defiant disorder, disruptive mood dysregulation disorder and childhood depression and anxiety can all mimic bipolar disorder in children.

Children with bipolar disorder can appear similar to children with ADHD because the limited concentration and high energy of ADHD seem like the symptoms of mania. Both conditions can make children irritable because their energy levels are out of their control. To tell the difference, look for specific mood states in which they appear hypomanic or manic for several weeks or months, as opposed to the more consistent patterns of ADHD.

Oppositional defiant disorder (ODD) is a behavior disorder of rule-breaking, irritability, and disrespect toward authority. It can look like either depression or mania, depending on the energy levels, but doesn't typically involve major changes to sleep or extremely high energy. In addition, ODD is usually brought on by family troubles or school problems such as bullying. With ODD, moods will usually last for minutes, hours, or weeks and be reactions to specific problems or irritants.

Disruptive mood dysregulation disorder (DMDD) is a disorder of temper tantrums. The child or teenager will overreact to frustration or not getting their own way. Although it's not easy to treat, DMDD will often respond well to parents taking a class in effective discipline. Another effective DMDD treatment is for the child or the entire family to go to therapy to improve the home environment and teach the child coping skills.

ADHD, ODD, and DMDD can all be comorbid with bipolar. The best thing to do is to accurately describe the child's moods, energy levels, and behavior to a good child psychiatrist or psychologist. Helping the child will also likely require change in other members of the family. Sometimes the only way to figure out the real diagnosis is for the prescriber to experiment with medications and find out what works.

Bipolar in Older Adults

If early care for bipolar disorder has gone well, the family has been able to relax for many years and the family member with bipolar has gotten to experience a satisfying adult life. But eventually, as that person's working years end and other health problems start to need attention, it will be time for the family to step up again and look at how they'll ensure safety and care for their family member with bipolar as they age.

Older adults have more problems with medication adherence. Some of it may be forgetfulness due to cognitive decline. Some may be hoping to do without medication if they've been stable for a long time. Because bipolar disorder doesn't really go away with age, this is a risky move and should only be done with the advice and assistance of the prescriber.

Mood states may change. Rates of comorbid anxiety disorders go down with age, so anxiety can be less of a problem. Some studies report a decrease in depression. Medications for bipolar appear to continue to work well for seniors but do have cognitive risks.

People with bipolar are more vulnerable to cognitive problems as they age. These include memory, executive functioning (planning and organization), processing speed (how fast they think), and attention. The parts of the brain responsible for these activities become smaller and less dense with age (fewer neurons). Early evidence suggests that this may be a long-term side effect of medication and/or metabolic syndrome (increased blood pressure, blood sugar, and weight gain).

As people age and begin to see multiple doctors who prescribe them medications for multiple conditions, there's a greater risk of accidental overdose or interaction effects (an individual medication that may be safe on its own, but becomes dangerous when combined with another medication). Every doctor should be aware of every medication the person with bipolar is taking, including over-the-counter medications, vitamins, or supplements.

Quality of life directly influences mood episodes. An active social and romantic life, interests, hobbies, and safe and happy living arrangements can have a measurable effect on how many mood episodes someone will have, which will then further affect their quality of life.

Hopefully, middle life will have offered a period of stability that gave caregivers some time with minimal responsibilities. But sooner or later, planning for late life will have to happen. Family members will need to plan living arrangements for the person with bipolar disorder as they age. In chapter 4, we'll start talking about group homes for people with mental illness.

Bipolar in LGBTQ+ Persons and BIPOC

Sara, a young Asian woman, was diagnosed with bipolar disorder. She felt that she had to keep it secret, because being open about it would embarrass her family and harm her reputation. The stress of trying to hide her mood episodes and appear "normal" caused comorbid anxiety.

Jeffrey, a young trans man, had been rejected by his family and became homeless. This made it nearly impossible to have stable sleeping and eating patterns and to access the care he needed. He had no real safety net. In addition, people used his bipolar disorder as an excuse to disrespect his trans identity, falsely claiming that it's a symptom. His experiences on the streets left him with comorbid PTSD.

Sean, a young black man with bipolar disorder, worked hard to appear "safe" to others, knowing that if he allowed any irritation or anger to show, many people would react to him as the stereotypical "angry black male." Because irritability is a more common symptom of depression in men, and Sean's impulsive behavior during mania would also be viewed through a racial lens, he carried a lot of guilt, anger, and self-blame about the social consequences of his symptoms.

Mental health disorders are already stigmatized. People with bipolar disorder need to be allowed to communicate openly about their disorder so that they can learn about their own patterns and let treatment providers know what they need. Some people work best with a therapist who shares their own background, or at least a therapist who is culturally sensitive enough to be able to talk about the interactions of race, sex, gender, and mental health.

Fear of stigma can prevent someone from getting treatment. Family members can help by being supportive of medication and therapy and helping find quality providers. People usually become more involved in and receptive to treatment if they have a good con- nection with their therapist or prescriber. The only exception to this is educational stigma, where a client with less education may not be as engaged in treatment as someone with more education. People in this position may need extra emotional support. Treatment pro- viders need to be clear that all people are welcome in their practice, and they must make certain to explain things in a way that clients can understand.

Now, it's time to get into the details of helping family members become part of a treatment team.

PART II

Beginning to Thrive: Treating Bipolar Disorder Together

Every family member will have intense thoughts and emotions about learning to live with bipolar disorder, and everyone will be affected in some way. Most of all, everyone will need places and times when they can be authentic about their feelings, both negative and positive. There will be loss (at least for a while) and there will be hope and change and discouragement and progress. Everyone will need a support system that meets their emotional and practical needs. In chapter 4, we'll work on bringing the family together as a team that can get the job done and support one another. In chapter 5, you'll learn about the different types of therapy that can help people with bipolar and support the family. In chapter 6, you'll learn about medications for bipolar disorder.

Dealing with a Diagnosis as a Family

Diagnosis can bring relief because it defines the problem. It can also bring anger, grief, resistance, self-blame, and conflicts regarding how problems should be handled. The family member with bipolar needs help, but each member of the family has important needs of their own as well. In this chapter, we will look at the emotional impact of a diagnosis and getting everyone the support they need.

The Emotional Impact of a Diagnosis

Tom showed signs of impulsiveness and mood changes. He was easily angered at times and wildly enthusiastic at others. He had been diagnosed with borderline personality disorder, but his new therapist felt that the mood changes weren't due to abandonment issues and didn't occur as quickly as is common in borderline. When Tom was referred for medication, the psychiatrist agreed that he could have a rapid-cycling bipolar disorder and put him on mood stabilizers, which started the process of stabilizing.

Treena had symptoms that caused her family anxiety, anger, and sometimes public embarrassment. When she received her bipolar diagnosis, it was straightforward, and she felt relieved. She took medication and attended therapy. Her family was still emotionally chaotic and she frequently went to stay with friends for a few days. Her family had to consult a therapist, as well as their family spiritual advisor, to help them express their anger and guilt before they could fully support her recovery.

As we learned, the diagnostic process is very in-depth. Over the course of the diagnostic appointment, the diagnostician (person who diagnoses) will ask your family member a lot of very personal questions. It's strange and uncomfortable to tell such personal information to a total stranger, but a diagnosis is only as good as the information it's based on. If your loved one decides not to share some information, they could end up with the wrong diagnosis, and thus with the wrong medications or therapy. Initial misdiagnosis is common, so encourage your family member to help the practitioner by openly and honestly sharing the information they ask for. If they don't feel comfortable with that practitioner, it is fine to find someone different to work with.

The diagnostician may also ask to speak to a family member or two. Family members can decide to be present for diagnosis, too, though if the person being diagnosed is an adult, they have the right to decide who can be present. If the person being diagnosed is under-age or has a legal guardian, it's still a good idea to get their agreement to having a family member present, so everyone feels comfortable. Accuracy is crucial, and emotional comfort is crucial to accuracy.

After the Diagnosis

Receiving an official diagnosis can create a lot of feelings. First, the positives: a lot of people feel hope and relief. Once you know what the problem is, a solution becomes possible. It may have previously felt like life would always be chaotic and difficult, but now you know that there is a path forward. Having a diagnosis can also be comfort-ing because there is less uncertainty about what's wrong. Because bipolar is strongly biological, diagnosis can be a relief because you know that the problem isn't anyone's fault.

It's also perfectly normal to have a lot of painful feelings. You might feel angry that you lived with chaos and uncertainty for such a long time. You might find yourself grieving things that you've lost in the past, like family events that went badly, or time your loved one spent in hospitals or jails that should have been spent at work, school, and with family. You might fear stigma or be afraid that the bipolar disorder may never truly stabilize. As you know, most people will eventually have long periods of stability, but there's no cure for bipolar disorder.

Sometimes the person with bipolar has hurt other family mem-bers with their behavior, and that must be addressed. Depression or mania can cause people to say terrible things and to do things that leave the family in a constant state of anxiety. There might be prac-tical consequences, too, like court dates or a lot of debt. Some family members may have had problems at work or school resulting from actions of the person with bipolar disorder.

Someone with a mental illness is not completely to blame for their behavior, but they are responsible for doing their best to get better (and most want to). During mania in particular, the parts of the brain that manage impulse control are not working. The bipolar family member has little to no control at that point. At the same time, family members will have experienced genuine loss because of bipolar disorder, and they deserve to have that acknowledged. It's healthy for both the person with bipolar and their family to acknowledge their desire to blame themselves and one another and do their best to cope with it.

It's helpful to shift your anger and blame onto bipolar disorder itself instead of the person with bipolar. The family can work together against the enemy of illness. In the future, one of you may even decide to write a book or blog about your family's "origin story." It can be a therapeutic way of expressing your feelings or letting go of a grudge. It can also be an act of service to help other people with mental illness or their families.

If family members aren't ready to be emotionally honest with one another, individual or family therapy can help. Now that you have the diagnosis, it's time to look at treatment options, get on the same page, and come up with a plan—but you have to do it together.

Accepting the Diagnosis

What if someone in the family isn't ready to accept the diagnosis? First, try to figure out why. The problem could be emotional or cultural, or there could be genuine questions about whether the diagnosis is correct. Sometimes it's a combination of those factors.

If you feel the need to argue with the diagnosis, ask yourself why. Start with "It can't be bipolar, because _____" and let the sentence end however you want it to end.

If you're experiencing emotional denial, the sentence will reflect anger, fear, embarrassment, or some other strong emotion. You might be angry at fate, the person with the diagnosis, or the professional who diagnosed your family member. You might not want it to be bipolar because you're afraid. If someone's actions during a mood episode have harmed you, it might feel like they're getting a "get out of jail free" card to deny responsibility.

You may also be very uncomfortable with the idea of a mental illness for cultural reasons, such as shame or stigma. You might also have spiritual or religious objections to the idea of a mental health disorder. It might help to remember that this is a biological disorder that, like a lot of biological disorders, is stress-influenced. It might also help to seek out community or spiritual leaders who are familiar with mental illness to see how you might balance your beliefs with the possibility that treatment can offer a better future.

But misdiagnosis *does* happen. So if you have specific concerns regarding the diagnosis, they're worth exploring. What symptoms have you seen that don't fit the description of bipolar disorder? What symptoms of bipolar aren't present in your family member? If you can list logical objections, it might be worth meeting with the person who gave the initial diagnosis or getting a second opinion.

Check-in

Use these prompts to help you get in touch with your feelings about diagnosis:

1. *The emotion I'm feeling is* _____ .

2. *Why do you feel this?*

"I'm feeling anger because she said terrible things to me and everybody's acting like that's okay because it's an 'illness.'"

"I feel hopeful because my child might finally get better and guilty that I'm exhausted from taking care of him. I feel like I shouldn't be angry at him for behavior that's caused by an illness."

Hospitalization

Kerry, a young woman in her 20s, was taken to the emergency room by her mother. Her mother was afraid because Kerry was staying up all night, using much more alcohol than usual to try to slow down, and displaying other signs of a manic episode. During past episodes, she had gotten into a car accident due to reckless driving. At the ER, Kerry was given a sedative, but it didn't touch her energy levels. She had a hard time sitting still and controlling her desire to play with the machines around her. After midnight, she was finally admitted to the psychiatric unit and given a dose of lithium to begin bringing down the mania. Still, it would be three days before Kerry slept, despite taking tranquillizers every night.

The thought of a psychiatric unit is scary, for valid reasons. The most important thing to remember about hospitalization is that we hospitalize someone only when it's necessary to keep them alive or safe. The words to know are "harm to self or others." Is your loved one currently a physical safety risk to themselves? Are they displaying suicidal behavior, risking their life with impulsive adventures, or starting fights? Are they a physical danger to others? If you can answer these questions with a "yes," then getting them to the emergency room is a good choice.

If your family member requires hospitalization, you may be feeling anger, fear, or guilt. For the moment, try to focus on what needs to be done.

If your loved one is willing to go to the hospital, driving them there is a good idea if your insurance doesn't cover an ambulance. If you have to hospitalize them involuntarily, calling the ambulance is generally better than calling the police. Paramedics usually have better training in mental health than police officers. If someone is violent, of course, you may feel you have no option but to call the police.

Whoever accompanies the bipolar family member to the emergency room may have a long, frustrating wait ahead of them. Because patients are treated in order of severity, rather than the order they arrived in, it can take a long time to get care. People with life-threatening injuries or illnesses are typically seen ahead of people with non-life-threatening conditions, so bring things to keep you both occupied. Don't forget their ID, insurance information, and a list of their current medications (psychiatric and medical), including any vitamins and other supplements. Make sure that when they're admitted, your loved one signs a release of information for at least one family member so that person can communicate with staff.

If your family member is admitted, make sure you plan a way to relax and treat yourself with self-care as soon as possible afterward. Don't feel guilty if you feel some relief that your part is over for now. You helped them get care from medical professionals, which is nothing to be ashamed of.

A psychiatric unit will manage any risks and prescribe medication. There are also therapy groups, but hospitalization is mainly about safety and stability. If you look at it that way, it can help you have realistic expectations.

Psychiatric hospitals can be scary, especially if it's someone's first time. Other patients' behavior can be frightening or hard to understand. The safety rules on a psychiatric unit are stricter than in other areas of medical care, so it's easy to feel trapped. Hospitals usually have rules about what objects patients are allowed to have, so ask before you bring photos, stuffed animals, or other family mementos.

Your loved one will receive a medication evaluation. If a family member wants to be included, make sure it's covered in the release of information, and that you leave a message for the psychiatrist letting them know to include you.

Some psychiatric units are safer and give better quality care than others. If you have a choice of hospital, check out their local reputation with your psychiatrist, therapist, or online. It's best to do this before an emergency happens, so that you're making those decisions with a calm mind and not when you're worried and in a hurry.

You can ensure the best quality of care for your family member by calling often, having a release of information to talk to staff, and visiting regularly. Make sure you know the visiting hours for the psychiatric unit. They are usually different from those of other units because of therapy group scheduling.

A patient has a legal right to communicate with people outside the hospital. Your family member will have access to a phone, but maybe not during therapy groups. Because of the confidentiality of health information, cell phones are usually not allowed. Patients in hospitals can also send mail. They may not have access to email.

If you have a release of information or if you are the patient's legal guardian, you have a right to information from staff, but you don't have a guarantee that they will respond to your questions immediately. They're allowed to call you back later as long as you eventually get that information.

The family can use the time during a hospitalization to rest physically and emotionally and work on family communication. If things have been emotionally fraught everybody, including the person who is hospitalized, may feel good about getting a break. There's nothing to feel guilty about.

Looking at Treatment Options Together

Right now, there is no cure for bipolar disorder. That could change in the future, but today, this is a lifelong diagnosis. The well-being of the person with bipolar should be the first priority for everyone's sake, but other family members will have their own needs and opinions.

The path to finding the right treatment is long and usually starts with medication. Bipolar I is nearly impossible to stabilize without medication. You may have family members who object to chemicals or are concerned about the greed of pharmaceutical companies. That's a discussion for another time: stability first.

If the diagnosis is bipolar II or cyclothymia, medication may be optional. If there are safety risks in either the depression or the hypomania, it's best to prioritize safety and monitor medication along with your practitioner. The realities of bipolar as a biological illness need to take priority over private opinions. You will disagree with one another; try to be supportive of openness but keep your priorities in order.

Treatment for bipolar disorder is a long-term process. At best, it can take months to achieve any kind of stability. For some, it may take years. Open communication with one another and your treatment team will help a lot, especially when something isn't working out well.

Most people need to try different medications before finding the right one. The first medication might not be effective, or the side effects may not feel tolerable. Therapists and prescribers vary a lot in their techniques and their ways of working with clients. They also retire, move, and get sick, so a change of providers is going to happen sometimes. Emotional support within the family is essential to dealing with changes in treatment.

Have an Action Plan

An action plan details exactly what each family member will do when certain symptoms begin to occur. For example, your family's action plan might say, "When Sam doesn't sleep all night and can't focus on work, Mom will call the doctor to make an appointment for a medication review." You'll need to know what hospital to go to in an emergency and what treatment options to pursue first. You'll need a computer or smartphone to look up local information and resources.

The best time to work on an action plan is when everyone feels calm. The family member with bipolar needs to be part of the planning, as do the family members most involved in day-to-day care. Invite other people with a stake in this to participate. If your family is having difficulty talking calmly about bipolar, you should include a therapist as an advisor and negotiator, especially if the person with bipolar requests the therapist's involvement. All providers should have a copy of the action plan.

You'll need to be honest with one another. What has been the most challenging part of treatment for each of you? What do you worry will happen? What do you think you might not be able to handle well? This is exactly what the action plan is for. As a group, make a list of situations you may need to handle, from a suicide attempt, to an angry family member, to someone in a manic episode getting the credit cards. Write down the problem and then discuss possible solutions. When you decide on the best solution (and maybe a backup plan), assign tasks to family members so that when something happens, you can check the action plan and put it smoothly into practice. A good action plan is supposed to get you through the toughest times and help you make the best possible decisions when emotions are running high and you're under pressure.

DEALING WITH DENIAL

What do you do when a family member isn't on board? Some family members may opt out of dealing with a diagnosis, and there might not be anything to do but respect that decision. If treatment goes well and life improves, they may decide to be more involved. If someone is too upset to contribute right now, the best thing for them to do is to stay outside the planning until they feel ready. When it's possible, leave the door open for someone to get involved once they're ready.

What if the person in denial is your loved one with bipolar? You always want that person involved, but if that's going to take a while the family should feel free to make important decisions without them, with the understanding that they're always welcome to change their minds and get involved.

Coping with a Diagnosis as a Family

Getting used to a diagnosis is never easy. But there are ways to make the process smoother and keep your family life steadier. Try these 10 tips to help everyone cope, communicate, and work together:

1. Leave room for respectful disagreement.

2. Be honest about your feelings.

3. Give family members who have legitimate grievances a chance to be heard.

4. At the same time, be solution-focused: What will get the person with bipolar closer to stability?

5. Assign specific jobs so that everything gets done and people aren't stepping on one another's toes while trying to do the same job differently.

6. Remember that negativity, criticism, and abuse really do make symptoms worse.

7. Plan fun family activities as often as you can.

8. Remember that family members other than the one with bipolar disorder have needs, too.

9. Remember that, as upsetting as the symptoms of bipolar are, they are caused by a biological illness over which your family member has limited control.

10. Avoid having one family member do all the work if you can. It's too exhausting for them.

DO THIS TOGETHER

Call a family meeting to discuss the action plan. Each family member who wants to be included should answer the following questions:

1. What are the situations that have been most difficult for you?
2. What do you need to change about this situation?
3. How has it affected you emotionally?
4. What can you realistically contribute to the care of the family member with bipolar?

Discuss everyone's thoughts and find some compromises.

Get Informed and Get on the Same Page

Share the information in this book with every family member who is willing to be involved. Do the exercises together and share your answers. Work toward crafting the answers into an action plan that addresses everyone's concerns.

Taking care of yourself and relaxing will be important, too. How can you make family meetings easier on everyone? Can you make it feel more relaxed by ordering in or cooking together beforehand?

Check in with one another often. Maybe have coffee together and ask how everyone's doing.

Stay open to healthy disagreement. Often, people only shout when they fear they won't be heard any other way. Encouraging people to disagree openly but respectfully can help calm down any problems.

Most of all, keep recovery and stability front and center. This will mean compromising with other involved family members. You may not agree with everything on the action plan, but if it's a compromise that allows everyone to get enough of what they need, roll with it so everyone can be on the same page when it's time to act on the plan. A crisis is no time for anyone to go off and do their own thing. When things are at their hardest, that's when family is the most valuable.

Remember, the Person You Love Hasn't Changed

Though mood episodes are frightening, remember that people with bipolar disorder do become stable again. You've probably heard of celebrities with bipolar disorder. You can read about the tough times they go through, so you know that it's possible to have bipolar disorder and still have a rich and meaningful life. There is hope for the family member with bipolar, though their life may look very different than previously anticipated. Bipolar disorder is only part of who they are. What else do you know about them? They're still the same person; the illness is the only thing that has changed. They still like a lot of the same things and have the same personality and interests.

Bipolar disorder might put a strain on your relationship. Do the things that you enjoyed before the diagnosis as often as you can. Maintaining some kind of a normal life is as important (and much more fun) as coping with your loved one's bipolar. If you have time and your loved one is well enough, follow up a doctor's appointment with a movie you both like, or something similarly enjoyable. They're still in there.

We've talked about some things that therapists can contribute when coping with bipolar disorder. In the next chapter, we'll look at how to find a good therapist and different types of therapy.

CHAPTER 5

Exploring Therapy Options Together

You've seen a lot of suggestions for coping with bipolar disorder already, and you might be feeling overwhelmed. You don't have to do it all alone. Therapy can help. Not only will a therapist benefit your loved one with bipolar disorder, but caregivers and other family members also have legitimate needs that a therapist can help with.

Why Therapy?

Therapy—a form of treatment based around talking rather than medication—can help people with bipolar disorder develop a more stable lifestyle. It can also help give them emotional support, spot a mood shift early, and reduce stressors. Therapy can cover a wide variety of issues and treatments, including learning more about bipolar disorder, skills training for handling arguments and other difficult relationship issues, managing strong emotions, building stronger family bonds, and putting together the action plan for and handling emergencies.

Family therapy can help everyone develop better communication skills, manage their emotions, learn about bipolar disorder, and put the action plan together. Individual family members might decide to get a therapist to help them process emotions and cope with caregiver stress. Caregiver support groups can also be helpful.

A combination of therapy and medication usually results in better treatment outcomes than medication alone, especially for bipolar I. If this seems hard to believe, think for a moment about some of the problems that bipolar has caused for your family that medication alone won't fix, such as hurt feelings and missed opportunities. In addition, therapy can be cost-effective for families because the money spent on therapy is often offset in other areas, like reduced time in hospitals, reduced debt, and fewer lost work hours.

The following are a few types of therapy that can help with bipolar disorder.

Cognitive Behavioral Therapy

Cognitive behavioral therapy (CBT) is based on the idea that our thoughts influence our feelings, and when our feelings change, our behavior changes. For example, if you feel hopeless about recovery from bipolar disorder, you'll act differently than if you believe that recovery is possible. CBT helps people change the thoughts that feed into their feelings, creating more positive outcomes.

Many people feel hopeless about the possibility of recovery. You may be worried that your family member will always be as chaotic as they are now. Their therapist could start by showing you both examples of real change in people with bipolar. Through treatment, the thought "This is hopeless" becomes "This might actually work," and feelings become more optimistic. More optimistic feelings help your loved one act in ways that lead to greater stability.

You can also start trying out some new behaviors. The therapist might recommend a change in the way you communicate about bipolar disorder. This change—if it works—can help you rethink your attitude and start to feel more optimistic.

CBT can lengthen the time between mood episodes, reduce the symptoms of depression and the severity of mania or hypomania, and improve social functioning. In pediatric bipolar, CBT improves attendance at therapy, increases satisfaction with therapy outcomes, and reduces severity of mania and depression as reported by parents of children and teenagers with bipolar disorder.

CBT can also reduce depressive and anxious symptoms, as well as negative emotions, among caregivers.

Dialectical Behavior Therapy

Dialectical behavior therapy (DBT) is a blend of CBT and mindfulness. DBT training involves four skill modules: distress tolerance, interpersonal effectiveness, mindfulness, and emotion regulation. While it was designed to treat borderline personality disorder, it's effective for several different psychological issues. Because borderline and bipolar share so many symptoms and are often comorbid, it's natural to ask whether DBT would be effective as a treatment for bipolar disorder.

There isn't a lot of research on the use of DBT for bipolar disorder, but what exists looks promising. In a study of adolescents with bipolar disorder, DBT increased attendance at an outpatient therapy program, reduced symptoms of depression, and decreased their frequency of suicidal thoughts. In adults, DBT decreased emotional instability and impulsiveness. DBT has also been successful in reducing depressive symptoms in adults.

There's not much research on DBT specifically for caregivers of people with mental illness. However, in research on caregivers of people with physical illnesses, DBT has also been useful for reducing caregiver stress by helping people manage emotions, cope with stress, and learn new interpersonal skills.

Mindfulness

Don't let the trendiness of mindfulness make you underestimate it. Mindfulness can be very helpful for a number of issues, including bipolar.

There are two components to mindfulness: mindful meditation and mindful awareness, both of which are intended to promote peace of mind and the ability to separate from your thoughts and feelings and not react to them. Mindful meditation is a complex topic. The short version is that you sit or lie quietly, focusing all your attention on your breath or on a mantra, which is a word or phrase that you choose to repeat, such as "OM" or "Calm." All of your thoughts and feelings will still be there. The goal is to recognize their presence but return your attention to your breath (or mantra), allowing thoughts, feelings, and urges to pass in and out of your awareness without reacting to them.

In this way, you learn to resist by not resisting. You can experience these mental events and still be at peace. You might think "This meditation is stupid and I must look like an idiot." You acknowledge the thought without judgment, seeing the thought as something separate from you, as if it were an object at a store that you aren't interested in buying. After briefly acknowledging the thought, you go back to focusing on your breath or your mantra.

Mindful awareness is a little bit different. You focus all your attention on an activity. When you have a thought, feeling, or urge, you notice it without judgment and calmly return your attention to whatever you were focusing on. You can work this into your day easily by doing things like cleaning, working, or engaging in a hobby with total attention.

There are some positive results for including mindfulness as part of therapy for bipolar disorder. In people whose bipolar disorder is in remission (stable), it can reduce anxiety and leftover feelings of depression, help increase awareness of mood changes, and lead to improved social functioning. In patients who still had active symptoms, it was associated with increased positive emotion, lower physical signs of stress, and a lowered tendency to pursue grandiose and impulsive goals in mania.

Psychoeducation

Psychoeducation means learning about psychological problems. Teaching accurate information about bipolar disorder is an important part of a therapist's job. You're also doing psychoeducation right now by reading this book.

Group psychoeducation classes can do more than just teach facts. They can help people with bipolar disorder better accept their diagnosis, become more insightful about their own behavior, and feel more positive toward medication and other parts of treatment. Group psychoeducation has the advantage of increasing participants' feeling of social support. When family members are included, everyone's coping skills improve, and there is typically a shift to more problem-focused coping rather than emotion-focused coping.

You can also receive psychoeducation online (teletherapy or telehealth). This is great for people who can't get to an in-person group. People who took part in online psychoeducation groups reported reduced relapse, decreased number and length of hospitalizations, and also that they were able to stay in treatment, take their medication more reliably, and reduce their feeling of being stigmatized. Online psychoeducation for families also helps reduce relapse and hospitalization in the family member with bipolar, and participants reported increased knowledge and skills plus decreased caregiver stress.

Interpersonal Social Rhythm Therapy (IPSRT)

One of the most important goals when treating bipolar disorder is to help the client put together a regular schedule of sleep and social rhythms (daily activity). Disruption of someone's schedule, especially the sleep schedule, is one of the most damaging parts of bipolar, and reliable daily routines can help improve symptoms. IPSRT was designed to do this. IPSRT also focuses on helping with relationships by managing conflicts and teaching relationship skills, including how to heal interpersonal ruptures. IPSRT is often used as part of the Systematic Treatment Enhancement Program for Bipolar Disorder, or STEP-BD, which also includes CBT, family-focused therapy, and medication.

IPSRT addresses the three most damaging problems in the treatment of bipolar disorder: stressful life events (including relationship problems), not taking medications, and disruption in social rhythms, including sleep.

IPSRT can enhance one's life satisfaction and quality of relationships. Disruption of both relationships and social rhythms increases someone's risk of having another severe mood episode after they've been stable on medication and therapy. In bipolar II, IPSRT and medication have the greatest effectiveness, but some people were able to improve on IPSRT alone. Whether a person is given their preferred treatment also has an effect on how successful a treatment will be, so there's a better chance of achieving stability when the wishes of the client are taken into account.

In adolescents, IPSRT has improved symptoms of depression and mania and also improved social functioning. Treatment that targeted symptoms of depression seemed to get the best results.

Group Therapy

Like group psychoeducation, group therapy can be very helpful. Group psychoeducation and group therapy are a little different, though there can be some overlap between the two. Group psychoeducation is a class that teaches information and skills; group therapy is a place to get support and deal with emotions and stressful events. Some groups blend psychoeducation with therapy.

Group therapy often helps in different ways than individual therapy. With individual therapy, your main relationship is with the therapist; that relationship and the therapist's knowledge help you make change happen. In group therapy, you become part of a small community of people who discuss and learn from their shared experience. The focus isn't always on you, it's sometimes on other people in the group.

Often, the therapist is helping the group members change one another for the better, rather than being the source of the change. The biggest disadvantage of group therapy, especially supportive groups for caregivers, is that a group can be difficult to find.

Group therapy can help lengthen times between mood episodes and even reduce the risk that another hypomanic or depressive mood episode will happen. For caregivers, it can reduce their sense of burden, increase their knowledge about bipolar disorder, and increase their sense of self-efficacy (the feeling that you know what you're doing).

Check-in

What is the most difficult part of being a caregiver for the people in your family? Is it the time pressure, the stress of waiting for the next problem to happen? The sense that you don't really know what you're doing? Something else?

Write down a list of the top five biggest difficulties. Discuss the list with your own therapist or someone you trust, or write about the difficulties in your journal.

What about Family Therapy?

There are a few different types of family therapies for bipolar disorder, so it's important to define your goals at the beginning. Different family members might have different goals, so make a list of what everyone needs and find the best match.

Family psychoeducation provides more information about what bipolar is and how to understand a loved one's diagnosis and symptoms. For children with bipolar disorder, family psychoeducation can help families feel more knowledgeable about bipolar and can help reduce expressed emotion in the household. Benefits from family psychoeducation are greater when the psychoeducation starts earlier in the disorder's progression.

We've already talked a lot about expressed emotion in the family and how higher expressed emotion can lead to worse outcomes for the family member with bipolar disorder. Expressed emotion can be difficult to change. In one- or two-session psychoeducation programs, psychotherapy did not result in any significant changes of expressed emotion. Longer-term family therapy is more successful. Some members might need individual therapy to work on caregiver stress or other issues in order to help change expressed emotion.

Psychoeducation groups can last anywhere from 8 to 14 weeks. This length can be very helpful because you have a chance to go home, try things out, and then go back to the group and share feedback with one another. It's a good way to translate advice from a book into real life and compare notes with others.

Family therapy doesn't normally have a specific end date. Instead, you'll set goals in the first couple of sessions. Therapy ends when the goals are met. A family may meet weekly at first, then switch to once every two weeks when they're making progress, then meet once a month for a few months as a check-in before ending therapy. Either the therapist or the family can decide to bring up the possibility of meeting less often.

The family therapist should not be anyone's individual therapist. It can sabotage the therapy if anyone feels like the therapist is biased, or if a family member asks the therapist to keep an important secret from the rest of the family.

If you have children, family therapy may touch on things you feel they shouldn't be involved with. That might be a good time for the child to have their own individual therapist or to spend some time with some other supportive person.

Family-Focused Therapy

Family-focused therapy (FFT) is a specific type of family therapy for bipolar disorder that focuses on problem-solving, improving communication, and psychoeducation. Family members with bipolar disorder should be part of FFT. It has strong research support, especially for improvement in depressive episodes. Family-focused therapy has also helped reduce symptoms of depression in caregivers.

Putting Together a Treatment Team

Ideally, a treatment team includes an individual therapist for the person with bipolar disorder, a family therapist to help the family learn about and adjust to the presence of bipolar disorder in the home, and a psychiatrist or advanced practice nurse to prescribe medications (for information about finding practitioners who fit your needs, see page 20). Other family members might have individual therapists as needed. The person with bipolar disorder and each family member who acts as a caregiver should be part of an online or in-person psychoeducation group if that isn't being covered in family therapy.

If the family member is dealing with bipolar disorder that is more severe and not yet stabilized, there are day programs for therapy groups, psychoeducation, and skills building. Clients are there for most of the day a few days a week. Some of these programs are called intensive outpatient programs (IOPs). If the program is run by a hospital, there may be a day program called a partial hospitalization program (PHP), in which patients are at the hospital for therapy groups during the day but live in their own homes at night. PHPs have the advantage of psychiatrists being available on-site.

Day programs usually have social workers and case managers who can help people sign up for services like Medicaid or Medicare, disability benefits, and other community resources. Many also have supported employment programs for anyone whose mental illness is severe enough that they will need extra help finding and keeping employment.

There are times when having someone with bipolar live at home with family is no longer realistic, and the person is not ready to live on their own. In that case, a group home might be an option. A group home is a long-term residence where several people with mental illness share a house and have staff to help them manage daily life. They're often found in or near large cities and can be a lifesaver when the family can't take care of someone in the home. Group homes are usually a part of larger community health organizations that also offer day programs and supported employment.

As with any other psychiatric care, quality varies a lot. In addition to visiting day programs and group homes, families can do a little research online to see what the organization's local reputation is like.

Seeing a General Practitioner

Your general practitioner should be aware of any mental health diagnoses that family members have and should have access to a list of their psychiatric medications. The mind and body are linked, and just as disease and injury can cause stress, emotional pain can also manifest as physical pain or make a physical disorder worse. There are also interactions between medications to watch out for, and physical disorders can have symptoms that mimic mental health disorders (such as epilepsy occasionally mimicking mania).

Although it may save a lot of time and trouble at the beginning, it's not a great idea to have your general practitioner prescribe psychiatric medications. Different medications can have severe side effects, so it's best to let a specialist take care of it.

Committing to Therapy

It can take a long time to get results in therapy. First, you need to get an accurate diagnosis. Then, there's usually a trust-building stage. This can be a good time to work on specific skills or to manage immediate risks for the family member with bipolar disorder. In therapy for caregivers, skills practice and handling immediate problems can be good places to start.

Therapy also won't be a completely linear process. There will occasionally be bad days and life events that cause setbacks. If you go in accepting that the occasional setback is part of the process, it's easier to stay solution-focused when that happens.

It's natural to be initially hesitant to tell a therapist everything. You'll feel nervous, embarrassed, relieved, and a lot of other things during the first sessions. When a therapist is trying to gather basic information or find out whether there are any serious risks to manage, please be honest. Even though it's difficult, being completely honest up front helps the therapist get the diagnosis right and keep all family members safe. If you or any family member has suicidal thoughts, substance abuse problems, or the urge to harm yourself, this needs to come up in the first session, so that you have your therapist supporting you from the start.

If anything goes wrong (scheduling conflict with a regular appointment, not feeling comfortable, becoming upset over something the therapist said or did), please talk to the therapist about it before giving up on therapy. If the therapist wants to talk about emotions when you feel desperate to learn some useful skills or some other difference in priority, please feel free to bring it up. A good therapist will treat it as normal and be willing to talk about it. The only exception would be if you feel that the therapist did something extremely unethical.

There are also times when therapists misspeak, forget things, are a few minutes late, or have other small problems. While it's not okay for them to consistently treat you as unimportant, they are human and make mistakes, and life happens to them just like anyone else. If your therapist made a normal human mistake that made you feel hurt or angry, feel free to bring it up in session and decide together how to handle it. It can even be a great exercise in assertiveness, conflict resolution, or relationship skills.

DO THIS TOGETHER

Go to one of the therapist directories listed in the Resources section (page 150). Look for "therapist bipolar disorder" and your zip code. You can also add a specific treatment, like FFT or CBT.

How many therapists did you find? If you live in an urban area, there are probably a lot. Do you have any specific traits you'd like your therapist to have, such as a certain gender, race or ethnicity, or religion? Use that to narrow down your options. Also check to make sure they take your insurance.

Narrow your search until you have two or three options. If you live in a rural area, that might not take long. Now, use a search engine to find your state's licensing board or department of professional regulation. Look for a license search. Put each of your possible therapists through the license search to see if they have a disciplinary history.

All good? Great. Now send each therapist an email or make a phone call requesting to talk for 15 or 20 minutes to get to know them.

During the consultation, ask any questions you want about their training and experience, how they work with bipolar disorder, and any other concerns you have. If you really like them, you can make your first appointment. Otherwise, feel free to have consultations with your other candidates before you decide. Don't forget to bring an ID, insurance card, and a credit or debit card to your first appointment.

Now that we've looked at therapists, it's time to learn about medications and add a prescriber to your team.

CHAPTER 6

Common Medications

To medicate or not? With bipolar disorder, it's a valid question. For some, medication is literally a lifesaver. For others, it's necessary but creates some new issues. And for some people with milder forms of bipolar disorder, medication isn't needed as long as they have a good plan for managing symptoms.

In this chapter we'll look at the medications for bipolar disorder and their most common side effects. We'll talk about getting used to medication as well as figuring out which side effects can be tolerated and which require calling the doctor for an adjustment. This chapter is a broad overview and isn't meant to replace medical advice. It's designed to inform and help you ask more thoughtful questions at the psychiatrist's appointment. Medications can affect people in very individual ways, so having the personal attention and knowledge of your loved one's doctor is the best way to make decisions.

The Role of Medication

Different types of bipolar disorder have different relationships to medication. For bipolar I, medications are essential, because both mania and depression can involve safety risks and limited control over behavior. A patient is unlikely to achieve any permanent stability without medication.

For some people with bipolar II, medications are optional. Because hypomania is less severe than mania and often enjoyable, people who experience it may be reluctant to try medication. But depressive episodes can still be incredibly dangerous for people with bipolar II. At least 25 percent of people with bipolar disorder attempt suicide, and almost exclusively during a depressive episode.

Cyclothymia involves milder forms of both depression and hypomania. It's the type of bipolar most manageable without medication. But medication is still a valid option if cyclothymia is causing someone to suffer.

Generally, prescribers try to manage the disorder with only one medication (monotherapy). They combine medications (polypharmacy) only if monotherapy isn't working. Doctors make medication decisions based on the patient's diagnosis, the kind of mood episode the patient is experiencing at the time of the appointment, and any potential safety risks, such as violence or suicide. If any other family members have bipolar disorder and have successfully controlled it with medication, psychiatrists may ask about which medications were effective for those family members.

Medication guidelines also differ based on the age of the person with bipolar disorder. If your loved one is a child or teenager, seek out a psychiatrist who has experience with pediatric bipolar disorder. If the patient is a senior, a psychiatrist with a specialty in geriatrics might be ideal. Medication recommendations for seniors are similar to those for younger adults, but with additional attention to side effects and interactions, due to the greater likelihood of comorbid medical disorders.

The medications most often used for bipolar disorder are mood stabilizers. As the name suggests, they're supposed to keep moods stable, with no escalation into mania or hypomania and no downslide into depression. Mood stabilizers can have a number of side effects, however.

Anticonvulsants, which are medications used to prevent seizures, also treat bipolar disorder. Depending on someone's symptoms, other medications can also be used, including antipsychotics and antidepressants.

All these medications are very powerful. Before filling the first prescription, be sure that your family member understands the most likely side effects and what to do if side effects show up. If they aren't stable enough to participate on that level, a family member should be present at appointments with the psychiatrist to ask detailed questions. If the person with bipolar disorder isn't consistent about taking medication right now, mention that to the doctor. Some medications come in an extended release form that doesn't have to be taken every day.

Lithium

Lithium has a history going back to ancient Greece, where physicians recommended that people with what we now call mania should visit hot springs, many of which had lithium in the water. It was introduced for psychiatric use in the United States in 1949, making it one of the earliest psychological drugs, but it wasn't approved by the FDA until 1970.

Lithium is one of the most effective medications for bipolar disorder and comes in several forms, including an extended release version. It does have an extensive list of side effects, including weakness, dizziness, weight gain or loss, damage to the liver and kidneys, and a form of diabetes. It may also cause skin problems. If your family member is taking lithium and experiencing side effects that are different or more severe than what you were told to expect, call the doctor immediately.

Don't panic at the list of side effects. Not every person who takes lithium experiences every side effect. Side effects are often dose-dependent, meaning that the higher the dose, the worse the side effects. Monitor side effects and contact the doctor right away if you have any concerns.

Anyone using lithium will need to take regular blood tests to make sure that their lithium levels aren't becoming high enough to do damage to the liver and kidneys. At first, the blood tests may happen as frequently as once a week, while the doctor looks for the lowest dose that will work for that person. After that, blood tests will become more and more infrequent. If someone taking lithium has a fear of blood or needles, a therapist should be able to help.

Other Mood Stabilizers

Carbamazepine (Tegretol and others) can be used to treat both seizures and bipolar disorder. Side effects include short-term light-headedness, sleepiness, and nausea. Liver and blood cell abnormalities are also possible, so anyone taking it will need regular blood tests.

Divalproex (Depakote, Depakene, and others) is another medication initially used to treat epilepsy. Research suggests that it's best for acute mania and not as useful for depression or maintenance treatment. Side effects include upset stomach, sleepiness, mild tremors, increased appetite, and weight gain. Liver damage is a risk, so regular blood tests will be needed.

Anticonvulsants

Lamotrigine (Lamictal) was originally prescribed to treat seizure disorders. But doctors and patients noticed that patients who took it showed improvement in mood, eventually leading to its use as a mood stabilizer. The most common side effect is skin rash, although even that's rare. Otherwise, the side effect profile is less severe than that of many other mood stabilizers. Blood tests are not typically needed for lamotrigine, unless it's taken with other anticonvulsants.

Topiramate (Topamax) may be helpful for managing mania. Unlike most of the other medications, it doesn't usually cause weight gain. Side effects include sedation, dizziness, slowed thinking, and memory difficulties. It's not recommended for people with kidney stones.

Antipsychotics

Antipsychotics are most often used in combination with mood stabilizers to treat psychotic symptoms during mania. Antipsychotics reduce hallucinations and delusions. Hallucinations are rarer in bipolar disorder than delusions, but they do occur sometimes. Antipsychotics can also be used as sedatives. Less often, they're used as mood stabilizers for people who don't tolerate other mood stabilizers well.

The most common antipsychotics for bipolar disorder are clozapine (Clozaril), quetiapine (Seroquel), aripiprazole (Abilify), olanzapine (Zyprexa), and risperidone (Risperidal). Their most common side effects are tardive dyskinesia (repetitive, involuntary movements) and other involuntary movement, drowsiness, and weight gain. Antipsychotics have been associated with the development of type 2 diabetes.

Antidepressants

Antidepressants are rarely used on their own for bipolar disorder since they've been known to stimulate manic episodes, even in people who typically experience hypomania and have never had a manic episode before. They can be used in combination with mood stabilizers to help manage symptoms of depression.

The most common antidepressants are bupropion (Wellbutrin), fluoxetine (Prozac), paroxetine (Paxil), sertraline (Zoloft), and venlafaxine (Effexor). Common side effects include increased appetite and weight gain, fatigue, nausea, and sexual side effects including loss of desire, erectile dysfunction, and decreased orgasm.

Medical Cannabis

Many people are curious about whether medical marijuana can be helpful for bipolar disorder. We've already talked about some of the risks of cannabis, such as the potential for earlier first mood episodes and a more severe course of treatment, particularly if the cannabis is used at a young age. Currently, there's no evidence that marijuana has any benefits as a treatment for bipolar disorder, and current research supports the idea that continued, frequent cannabis use can actually make symptoms worse over time. The research is also not very specific about strains of marijuana or specific individual components, like THC or cannabidiol (CBD). Right now, it looks like the risks outweigh any medical rewards.

DO THIS TOGETHER

There are a few different ways to learn about medications. Drugs.com and Healthline are good sources of information. If someone in the family is comfortable reading research articles, you can look up medications on Google Scholar.

For any potential medication, make sure you can answer all the following questions:

- What is it supposed to treat? (Bipolar as a whole? Just the depression? Just the grandiose delusions during mania?)
- How long will it take to feel the effects?
- What side effects does it have?
- What should we do if it causes a side effect?

Managing Medication

Medications need to be monitored frequently at first, so that the prescriber can find the lowest possible dose that will still be effective. If medications are being managed outside the hospital, expect weekly blood tests as well as phone calls or emails regarding blood test results. Weekly in-person appointments are a possibility, too. Because each person's response to medication is individual and hard to predict, it's common to switch medications a few times if something isn't working or the side effects are too difficult. Use the chart on page 93 to track changes in symptoms and side effects. If there are any tremors, severe weakness or dizziness, or totally unexpected problems, get in touch with the doctor immediately or follow their directions for emergencies.

What It's Like to Be on Medication

Jaden had bipolar I. He went to the hospital with acute mania that included psychotic symptoms. He couldn't sleep and the staff had a hard time getting their work done when he was around, because he constantly interrupted them to talk about anything and everything. He even ate while pacing the floor for a few days, because sitting down for more than a minute was too difficult. That led to agitation with some of the other patients; he responded with a grandiose level of anger and entitlement when anyone tried to talk to him about it. His psychiatrist gave him a "loading dose" of a mood stabilizer to get control of the symptoms. It worked, but he began having severe side effects, including tremors, and his next blood test revealed near-toxic levels of the medication. The dosage was lowered and adjusted over the next few days, and he was released. Weekly blood tests continued for a while; eventually he only had to get a blood test once a month, and later only every few months.

Cristina, a woman on the same unit, came in with suicidal depression so severe that she had to be sedated for her own safety and watched by a staff member 24–7 for a few days until an antidepressant took effect. She started to show improvement and began to attend groups and make friends with other patients. But she became easily angered and frustrated. She drew all over the walls of her room with a marker she stole from the activity therapist. She was frustrated when staff were upset about it. She tried to explain her artistic vision, but her words made no sense.

Cristina slept for maybe two or three hours each night. A nurse let the psychiatrist know that Cristina appeared to be having a manic episode. This was the first sign that she actually had bipolar disorder instead of depression. Two different mood stabilizers failed to work, so the doctor switched her to an anticonvulsant. Cristina's mania finally began to calm down. Her doctor added an antipsychotic to address her unrealistic thinking and illogical speech. After a week she showed improvement, with only mild side effects. In total, it took slightly more than a month in the hospital to reduce symptoms and find a mix of medications that helped her stay stable and manage side effects.

Taking psychiatric medications is definitely not like taking aspirin for a headache. No two people are alike in how they respond. We don't always know exactly what a medication does to the brain, much less why the main effects and side effects vary so much in different people.

Some side effects are due to the fact that medication affects multiple areas in the brain, not just the ones related to bipolar. Changing the activity in parts of the brain is related to a decrease in bipolar symptoms. But changing the activity of those unrelated cells causes side effects.

As research on the brain progresses, we'll develop better knowledge about why medications work, exactly what they do, and how they'll affect a specific person. In time, there will also be new medications that are much more precise. But for now, we have to work with what we've got.

Check-in

Best practices recommend considering the opinion of the person with bipolar during treatment decisions as much as their current mental state allows. Before the appointment, a family member should sit down and ask them about any concerns and any values or beliefs they have about medications. If necessary, the family member should help the person with bipolar make a list of questions and act as an advocate during the appointment.

It Won't Work Right Away, and Not Everything Will Work

It takes up to a week for medications to start taking effect. Doctors can give a loading dose (a very large dose) of medication to speed this up, but as you can imagine, that has to be monitored carefully. It can take up to three weeks to see how a medication will work for someone, and there's no guarantee that the first medication a doctor tries will work.

Adjusting and Figuring Out What Works

You and your family will be less frustrated if you start off by expecting multiple changes and adjustments when it comes to medication. Sometimes someone gets lucky and discovers the right medication right away. But that isn't the norm and it's not fully under the doctor's control; it's the state of the research right now. Sometimes a medication might work but have intolerable side effects. Other times, a medication might be easy to tolerate but doesn't really solve the problem. For some people, it can take up to 18 months to find medication or a combination of medications that works with very few side effects.

Keep Track

Use the chart on page 93 to track changes in symptoms and side effects. Keeping a chart like this will help you spot changes over a few days, and if the family member with bipolar is comfortable keeping it someplace visible, it's an easy way to keep everyone in the loop on their progress. If someone's symptoms prevent them from keeping the chart at first, or if the person with bipolar is a child, another family member should help.

Managing Expectations

When will your family be able to go back to a "normal" life? That depends on how quickly the doctors find the right blend of medications and therapy. But it won't be right away. Some people with bipolar disorder will have a pretty normal life in which they work, have their own place, and have healthy relationships. Others will always need at least some help.

As mentioned in chapter 4, if someone isn't stable enough to go back to a normal work or school program, think about finding an intensive outpatient program (IOP), partial hospital program, or day program. If someone can't live alone and there isn't enough family support for them to live with family, look into group homes in your area. No matter what their current level of stability, someone with bipolar disorder needs a regular sleep schedule, a reasonably regular diet, and an emotionally supportive place to live. This is the foundation that medication and therapy will build on to create stability.

DO THIS TOGETHER

Here's an example of a week-long symptom and side effects chart to track responses to medications. The family member with bipolar disorder should fill it out daily until symptoms have been stable for at least a month on a medication that they're tolerating well.

On the left side, list specific symptoms of mood episodes, instead of overall mood (instead of writing "depression," write "fatigue, loss of pleasure, sadness, suicidal thoughts, and low sex drive"). Also list potential medication side effects.

Give each symptom a rating from 1 to 5 daily, with "1" meaning "severe" and "5" meaning "no important problems." If weight gain is a concern, weigh in only once a week to avoid obsessing about it, unless a doctor says otherwise.

MEDICATIONS:

	SUN	MON	TUES	WEDS	THURS	FRI	SAT
SYMPTOMS OF MANIA							
Amount of sleep							
Quality of sleep							
Spending							
Rapid speech							
Feelings of anger							
Feelings of confidence							
Flirting with strangers							
MEDS SIDE EFFECTS							
Weakness							
Dizziness							
Increased appetite							
Weight gain (1x/week)							

Going Off Medication and Medication Non-Adherence

At some point or another, your family member with bipolar will likely want to try life without their medications. Between the side effects, blood tests, remembering to take the medication regularly, and the feeling of having a chronic illness, it's an understandable desire. Because bipolar disorder comes with powerful moods and a pretty high fatality rate, however, it isn't a decision to take lightly.

A therapist becomes even more important during a change in medication, because they can help monitor the subtle signs of mood and behavior change. Meanwhile, a psychiatrist should advise the patient on the decision as well as what physical and psychological changes are normal and which might be signs that a serious problem is developing. In particular, ask if any of the medications are likely to have withdrawal effects or should be stopped slowly instead of all at once.

After talking over the risks and possible rewards with the prescriber, therapist, and any other stakeholders (like the family members whose help they'll need if they have a severe episode), if the person with bipolar still wants to try life without medication, do it carefully and in frequent contact with the therapist. The person with bipolar should start keeping a chart of changes in mood, sleep, appetite, and any other signs that a new mood episode is starting, such as an increase in spending or a sudden urge to join a few dating apps. It might be useful to keep the chart someplace where a family member and/or the therapist can help monitor changes, such as a shareable spreadsheet or app.

Make an agreement about how they'll know if it's time to end the experiment and go back on medication. Will they go back on medication if they start sleeping all day or having suicidal thoughts? If they start spending too much money? Exactly what changes in sleep would be a sign that the experiment is over?

If the experiment goes well and the person can live without medication, there will still be symptoms. The person with bipolar will need to be realistic about their needs and how to meet them. If their appetite is low during depression and they tend to under-eat, for example, they can buy a supply of shakes, bars, and other foods that don't need to be cooked so they can eat as easily as possible.

Sometimes someone will go off medication without medical supervision. This is dangerous but understandable. Side effects can be a big challenge, and people sometimes need to grieve before they can adjust to the idea of taking medication for the rest of their lives. People with hypomania often want the highs and the confidence back.

Still, there are risks to stopping without supervision. Withdrawal can make it hard to tell when symptoms of bipolar disorder are returning. Work and relationships might start to go downhill when symptoms return. If someone had used another substance like alcohol to manage symptoms in the past, that substance abuse problem could come back.

Often, people who stop taking medication are hoping that bipolar symptoms won't return. As hard as it is to hear, that's not realistic. There's no cure for bipolar disorder, so going off medication will mean that sooner or later (probably sooner), that person will need to figure out how to manage symptoms without it. Easing off medication with a doctor's supervision can make the process easier, so that there's as little risk as possible, and medication is easily available if it turns out that it is needed.

Part 3 will help you thrive as a family when loved ones have bipolar disorder. We'll talk more about how to track and prevent mood changes, be emotionally supportive of one another, and be an advocate for your family member (and for the community of people with bipolar disorder, if you want). Finally, we'll go into more detail about healthy boundaries and relationships.

Thriving as a Family

Part III focuses on creating support, building relationships, and taking care of yourself. Chapter 7 looks at catching problems early by tracking moods and knowing what to do when a new mood episode starts. Chapter 8 includes practical techniques for having difficult conversations and tough decisions about care. We'll also dive into ways to advocate for people with mental health issues. Chapter 9 talks about negotiating boundaries and respecting others' boundaries when relationships are in need of repair. It looks at how to take a team approach to important family decisions. Chapter 10 reminds everyone to be understanding and forgiving of yourself and your family: Real life is rarely as clear as it seems in a book, but most people with bipolar disorder will find stability.

CHAPTER 7

Getting Ahead of Moods

This chapter focuses on details that can move your family toward stability. You'll learn how to recognize mood episodes, how to track moods (and why you should), when to get help, and how seemingly small details like sleep and nutrition can play an important role in helping someone with bipolar disorder.

Mood Signs and What to Do

In one family, three different members had different types of bipolar disorder, all with different levels of severity. Because of this, they had varying needs. Jason has severe bipolar II. Even though he had found the correct medication, he still couldn't live independently, so he moved to a group home for people with mental illness. It can get chaotic there, but there are staff around 24 hours a day to help them. He attends a day program where he does group therapy and builds coping skills as well as an employment program that lets him have more independence and supplement disability checks. Jason's brother, Rick, developed bipolar I, and sometimes has to be hospitalized during a manic episode. Otherwise, he works, lives at home, and has a good social life with the help of medications and therapy. Jason and Rick's first cousin, Jada, developed bipolar II, has been hospitalized only once (for suicidal depression), and lives a stable life with the help of medication. She tried not taking medication, but the depression became unmanageable. She still misses the highs of hypomania, but hasn't been hospitalized in several years.

We've discussed the symptoms of the four different mood episodes (depressive, manic, hypomanic, and mixed). Now, let's talk about what they look like in everyday life.

Depression. Someone with a depressive mood might start out by feeling irritable, sad, or fatigued. They may spend more time around the house, lose their appetite, snap at people, or cry more easily. An event such as relationship stress or excessive drug use may trigger the episode. Not all depressions are triggered by circumstances, however.

Those suffering from depression may sleep most of the day, or get into bed after work and not come out until they have to. They may neglect to eat and lose too much weight, or eat comfort foods and gain too much. They may feel too fatigued to keep up their hygiene. They're likely to stop doing activities they enjoy and have a harder time making themselves get any work done. If they're in school, assignments may be late or they won't study as much as they should, and test grades will suffer. People with depression feel guilt when there's no reason for them to, and they feel self-hatred over mistakes that seem minor to others. If someone is powering through a depressive episode and getting everything done, it will be important to pay attention to irritability, crying, sleeping, and eating, because these may be the most visible signs.

Mania. Someone having a manic episode will barely sleep for days and still have enough energy to function. They may have trouble sitting down for very long, even at mealtimes. They'll often come up with unrealistically ambitious plans and then attempt to carry them out. They might start talking about becoming a musician (when they don't play an instrument or sing well) in the morning. By the time everyone's home from work, they have Twitter, Instagram, YouTube, and Twitch accounts; a new wardrobe; and a bass guitar. If someone tries to talk them down, they may get irritable or just ignore the critic. People with mania may drink or use drugs, spend money, have impulsive sex, or engage in other risky behaviors they wouldn't normally do. If they have psychotic symptoms, they may believe that they are someone powerful or famous (delusions), or they may have hallucinations or distorted vision and hearing.

If someone has very strong hallucinations and delusions outside a manic episode, they may have schizoaffective disorder, bipolar type. They'll probably be prescribed both a mood stabilizer or anti-convulsant and an antipsychotic.

Hypomania. Someone with hypomania can usually get by on a lot less sleep than normal—maybe four or five hours a night—for weeks at a time, without feeling any fatigue. During a hypomanic episode, they might work all day, go out for a few hours at night, sleep a few hours, and do it all over again, every night of the week. Their grandiosity will look and feel more like an intoxicating sense of confidence. They're less likely to make huge changes to their lives and more likely to be ambitious, sure of themselves, and take on bigger challenges than they normally would. They might go walking or running alone in the middle of the night, take on extra projects at work, or be a lot more flirtatious and charming than usual because they lack their normal inhibitions.

Not everyone with hypomania has fun with it. For some people, it still feels out of control. They can start feeling irritable and burnt out, but their high energy levels won't allow them to stop. Insomnia is sometimes worse than expected, and high energy can feel like anxiety or agitation. This is called "dysphoric hypomania."

Mixed episode. A mixed episode is when someone has both manic or hypomanic and depressed symptoms at the same time. They might have high energy and grandiosity, but also have sad and irritable moods. They can have racing thoughts, rapid speech, and impulsivity, but still have suicidal thoughts, guilt, and self-loathing. They might feel very good and very guilty at the same time. It can be hard to tell a dysphoric hypomania from a mixed episode, but in the end that problem doesn't matter as much as helping your family member get treatment for it.

Tracking Moods

Tracking moods can really help. Just like the medication chart in the previous chapter, a mood tracker can help you figure out which changes in therapy, medication, and lifestyle are driving the changes in mood. Some people's mood episodes even change seasonally, such as having a hypomanic episode every year in the fall. A tracker will help you stay on top of it all.

At the beginning of treatment, tracking moods will help you identify which symptoms change when a new mood episode is starting. Sleep is often one of the first things to change. You may notice a reduction in sleep over a few nights when a manic episode is starting, or that more naps than usual signal a shift toward depression. The details will be different for everyone.

Once you've identified the signs of a mood shift, you can let your treatment team know that a change is happening. You should also go over sleep schedules, nutrition, make sure medications are being taken at the same time every day, and check to see if there's any change in your family member's ability to manage work or school. Therapists can teach coping skills specific to the needs of your family.

Once someone is stable on medication, continue using a mood chart. After a few months of stable mood, you can probably complete it weekly rather than daily, until you notice a change that might be important.

For the first few months of stability, people with bipolar disorder and their families can overreact to every slight change in sleep or mood. In real life, everyone has the occasional night of bad sleep or the occasional irritable mood. The mood chart can help you avoid overreacting by checking to see if there have been other changes to mood or productivity, or if it's just something that happened.

DO THIS TOGETHER

To keep extra work to a minimum, you can use the symptom tracker from chapter 6 (page 93) to track moods as well. Make sure you have energy levels listed, along with all the initial signs of a changing mood. You can add emotions or emotional numbness.

There are plenty of great apps designed to track moods as well. Choose one that's flexible enough to meet most if not all your tracking needs, and read the reviews. Some of these apps are listed in the Resources section (page 150). In addition to looking at reviews for an app you're considering, check Google Scholar to see if any research has been done on the app.

The person with bipolar disorder isn't always the first to notice changes in their own moods or behavior. Sometimes family and friends will notice the outward signs first, so the mood tracker can include input from everyone. Whether you use pen and paper, a chart like the one in chapter 6, or an app, make sure that everyone who might need that information has easy access to it.

Knowing When to Get Help

Some people's moods change very quickly. Some go to bed in a depressive episode and wake up in a manic episode. Others see a slower mood shift. For some, it's predictable by season, or there's a specific stressor that usually brings on a depressive episode. Either way, it's important to know when to get help. The mood tracker will help you identify when it's time to seek professional help and enable you to recognize long periods of stability when it's okay to scale back your efforts.

Someone with mild depressive episodes might still occasionally have suicidal thoughts. This should always, without fail, be a sign that it's time to get help. Tell the therapist and prescriber immediately. The goal is to get the depression under control while the suicidal thoughts are still only thoughts.

How bad does mania have to be before you get help? Once you're certain someone is having symptoms of a manic episode (loss of sleep over several nights, spending more money, flirting more, or whatever their specific symptoms are), call the prescriber and the therapist. Since medication is more helpful than therapy for managing mania, the prescriber should be your first priority.

Help doesn't only come from professionals. It comes from family and friends as well. What does your family member need when they're having a depressive episode? Can their friends and other family members help with anything? Support systems can do a lot. Depression will lie to someone with bipolar and tell them (convincingly) that no one loves them or cares what's happening to them. Messages from the support system challenge that thinking, even when someone is too depressed to respond to those messages. It's also helpful if someone is willing to do some shopping, cooking, or simply spend time with the family member. Family and friends can also help during manic or hypomanic episodes. Friends might go out with someone to help them manage their impulsive hypomanic behavior, or organize activities to keep them at home and give them an outlet for excess energy. Exercise, art, and creative writing are common outlets. An outlet may not change the hypomania, but it will help keep someone safe from their own impulsivity. If someone spends a lot of money during mania or hypomania, a family member should keep the credit cards and make sure the person with bipolar disorder has enough cash to get through the day and that the bills are paid on time.

When there's a safety issue, it's best to get them to the hospital. If there's a realistic risk of suicide or violence, hospitalization is the best option.

All health-care professionals, including therapists, are "mandated reporters." A mandated reporter is someone who is required by law to report a risk of suicide or homicide, or the abuse of a minor, elder, or person with a disability. Bipolar disorder is considered a psychiatric disability, even if the person doesn't receive disability payments. If a mandated reporter becomes aware of an immediate threat of suicide, homicide, or abuse as previously described, they must legally report it to the authorities.

For risks of suicide, homicide, and some risks of violence (this varies by state), a person can legally be hospitalized against their will, but only if the risk is immediate. Immediate risk means that the person has the intention to attempt suicide now or within the next few hours and has the means to do so. Someone at immediate risk of suicide should never be left alone, not even to go to the bathroom. Someone who has suicidal thoughts but no intention of acting on them should never be hospitalized against their will, although that person can choose to voluntarily admit themselves to the hospital.

It can be hard to make decisions under the stress of an escalating mood. That's why it's so important to write down benchmarks in your action plan, such as "If Tim has two sleepless nights without feeling tired, we'll go to the doctor for a medication re-evaluation and I'll take away the credit cards." or "If Nora misses three assignments in a week and goes to bed early, or feels fatigued for at least three days, we will tell her therapist and psychiatrist." Once someone meets a benchmark, the family should take the planned action.

Is It Possible to Get Ahead of Moods?

You can minimize damage by keeping charts and acting on benchmarks, but can you change the fact that a mood episode is coming on? Sometimes. Usually, you can reduce the severity by monitoring several factors, including drugs and alcohol, expressed emotion, stressors, seasonal changes, and medications. Prescribers can adjust prescriptions to manage an oncoming mood. Depending on the symptoms, they can add antidepressants, antipsychotics, or sleep medications. You can also utilize one of the other most powerful tools you have: routine.

Put Together a Routine

Having a daily routine is part of managing symptoms. This part of treatment is called interpersonal and social rhythm therapy (see page 74 for more detail). IPSRT helps manage sleep, diet, work, the quality of personal relationships, and other details of a daily routine. A routine will also make it easier to notice when symptoms start to disrupt daily life.

Someone with bipolar disorder will need to take their diagnosis into account when they're planning their work life. They may need a job that allows them the flexibility to work harder during periods of hypomania and reduce hours during periods of depression. On the other hand, they'll need to make sure that the "flexible" schedule isn't making symptoms worse by breaking routines. Many people with bipolar prefer a job where they have to leave the house to go to work, but some flexible work-from-home options can be better for others. It helps to look back at the past to see what worked during schooling and at previous jobs, and what triggered symptoms.

Sleep

Since circadian rhythms affect symptoms, a regular sleep schedule is part of managing bipolar disorder. It doesn't have to be perfect; nothing will come crashing down if your family member goes to bed at 11:15 p.m. instead of 11:00 p.m. But sleep and wake times should be fairly consistent. In people who are euthymic (not having a mood episode right now), treating insomnia with cognitive-behavioral therapy reduces both insomnia and the number of relapses into mania or hypomania. More variation in the sleep-wake cycles leads to less stability of mood.

Insomnia is common in people with bipolar disorder, and not just during mania or hypomania. Insomnia can be a symptom of depression, and even people in a euthymic state have higher rates of insomnia than people who don't have bipolar disorder.

Start with basic sleep hygiene: Make sure your family member goes to bed and wakes up each day at a predictable time. Ensure medications are taken regularly so you can tell if they're altering sleep patterns. Urge them to use their bedroom only for sleeping or intimacy, and do not do anything physically active or watch anything overly exciting for at least half an hour before bed.

Learning to manage thoughts can help with insomnia. Meditation can help, but anything physically and mentally relaxing is good. They can try a safe space meditation (there are a lot of them on meditation apps and online), a sleep app, or CBT if the insomnia becomes chronic. For most people, the time before bed should be calm, quiet, and stress-free, but if your family member sleeps better with music or light, work with that. If there are any deeper reasons why they have trouble sleeping without lights or noise, a therapist can help explore those issues.

Keeping an Eye on Energy Levels

When someone has bipolar disorder, it might be necessary to structure the day around their energy levels. During a depressive episode, they might be able to get a lot done in the morning but need a nap just to function by afternoon. During mania or hypomania, there may be times of day when the impulsivity or high energy is at its peak. Lifestyle changes should be flexible enough to change as mood episodes do. This won't be as important once someone is stable on the right medications, but knowing typical daily changes in energy will still help identify an oncoming episode. When someone is trying to manage bipolar disorder without medications, charting energy levels will be one of their most important tools.

Putting energy levels on the mood tracker will help identify someone's typical patterns. At what time of the day is their energy usually the highest? Lowest? Changes in energy during the day are common in bipolar. During a depressive episode, they might have a brief period of higher energy in the morning when they can accomplish the most but be fatigued by afternoon, then have a burst of energy in the evening. During a manic episode, someone might function best during lower-energy times, when they can focus better.

If your family member is trying to manage bipolar without medications, charting energy levels can help plan work goals, social activities, and other daily life tasks. A low-energy time might be ideal for meditation, light yoga, or a relaxing hobby. Some people will need a nap during the day to function at their best.

Check-in

How is everyone feeling about the value of routine? Someone who's already stabilized may feel that life is too organized and they need safe ways to break the routine. Others might worry that IPSRT is an unrealistic ideal or think that routine couldn't have that big an impact.

Healthy Eating

People with chronic mental illness are more likely to eat excessively and eat a low-quality diet, which leads to higher rates of type 2 diabetes and cardiovascular disease. Some of this is due to medication: mood stabilizers, antidepressants, and antipsychotics all have weight gain as a side effect.

The field of nutritional psychiatry is new, but early research suggests that a healthy diet may have a positive effect on mood stability, possibly by reducing inflammation. Inflammation is the way that the body reacts to injury and infection in order to promote healing. In a visible wound, the heat, redness, and pain are signs of inflammation. In the brain, anything that causes inflammation could affect mental health. Researchers are trying to discover if good nutrition may reduce inflammation in ways that help mental illness. Psychological stress can cause inflammation as well, which may be one of the pathways by which stressors can make mental illness worse. Remember, though, that nutritional psychiatry is fairly new and not something to DIY at home. It's also not a complete answer to bipolar disorder; nutritional psychiatry is just one area of exploration for possible future solutions.

Ketogenic diets have been trending in psychiatry for a few years because they can help manage epilepsy, but the benefits for bipolar disorder are unclear. There have been a few success stories reported, but they're based on case studies (research done on only one person instead of on a large sample of people), so we don't know if the diet would be helpful to everyone with bipolar disorder.

Exercise

One of the hardest parts about exercise is having the motivation, especially during a depressive episode. Someone with bipolar disorder may need different styles of exercise for different mood states because of their varying energy levels.

While there are many personal stories about exercise helping with mood episodes, there's no evidence yet that it directly treats bipolar disorder. There is much evidence that aerobic exercise helps treat major depression, but there isn't enough research yet to prove that true for bipolar depression as well. The biggest benefit beyond general good health might be exercise's ability to offset the side effects of medications, such as weight gain.

Because exercise can help manage weight gain from medications but symptoms can also make it harder to exercise, help your family member make a list of barriers to exercise and think about how they can be solved. Barriers can be moods, energy levels, equipment available, boredom, or anything else that stands between your family member and working out. During a depressive episode, it will be harder for them to get motivated, so doing a fun exercise at home might be more realistic than going to the gym. During a hypomanic or manic phase, they might be prone to overdoing it and injuring themselves, so an exercise plan might help them know when to stop. If the family member with bipolar disorder feels lonely and unwanted, exercising with someone else might help. Linking the workout to something they already value can be helpful. If someone loves superhero movies, finding a superhero-themed workout online might help; if they enjoy dancing, buy a dance aerobics video.

"Routine" Doesn't Mean "Boring"

How can you make any part of the routine more fun or meaningful? Life with bipolar disorder is difficult enough without being boring about it. If your family member loves to cook, use that to help them eat healthy. If they hate to cook, work with it by finding affordable prepared foods. Encourage them to do exercise that's fun. Buy new sheets for the bed. Whenever possible, respect their energy levels and flow with them, not against them, until they can be stabilized.

It can be challenging to help care for someone with bipolar disorder. Chapter 8 will go into detail about how family members can support loved ones with bipolar disorder while still looking after their own well-being.

Supporting Someone with Bipolar Disorder

Bipolar disorder affects the whole family, which is why treatment often needs to include the whole family. This chapter is about making sure that everyone's needs are met, while avoiding emotional toxicity as much as possible.

Supporting One Another

Jean and Scott raised their son Henry in a safe home in a safe neighborhood. He was a well-behaved high school student who had good grades, good friends, and a social life that wasn't wild enough to cause his parents any concern. So when he had to leave college in his second semester and move back home because of the onset of bipolar disorder, it was a shock. There was a family history of bipolar and epilepsy, though neither of his parents had bipolar. They had hoped the cycle was broken by their love and the safe home they provided.

Henry's first episode was mania, which helped him get an accurate diagnosis fairly quickly. However, finding the right medication was a challenge. The whole family had to live with the consequences of his manic symptoms. He would become irritable, impulsive, and demanding, and his high energy was difficult to cope with. The family would ask and then order him to calm down. Henry embarrassed them in front of neighbors and family, and their attempts to manage his behavior with rules and consequences failed epically and sometimes publicly. He got angrier and angrier when they couldn't understand that his body wouldn't let him do as they wanted. Henry felt blamed and judged. Jean and Scott felt inadequate and angry and grieved the loss of their pre-bipolar life. An hour of quiet would have been nice. Eventually, Henry's psychiatrist found the right mix of medications and he began to stabilize, but not before some emotional rifts had developed that would take time to heal.

It is important to understand that someone with bipolar disorder has little to no control over their behavior, especially during mania and severe depression. During hypomania, mild depression, or cyclothymia, it can be easier to channel that behavior into less damaging paths. But someone with bipolar disorder can't just stop their symptoms any more than someone with a head cold can stop sneezing. Even the lifestyle choices recommended in chapter 7 are unrealistic without the right treatment and an emotionally safe home environment.

Someone with bipolar disorder needs their family to understand how out of control they are. The symptoms are not fun and they are not choices. Bipolar symptoms are a runaway train and your family member is a passenger, just as you are. On the surface, there can be a lot of conflict between the person with bipolar disorder and the rest of their family. However, the conflict is really with the illness, and the whole family is in that conflict together.

Supporting someone with bipolar disorder can be difficult and frustrating. There are a few things you can do to be supportive: You can manage your own emotions, assist your family member with things they currently can't do for themselves, and help avoid the consequences of their actions.

Managing emotions means admitting your feelings and finding an outlet for them. You will feel angry. Try to direct your anger at the illness—not the person with the illness—and be honest with yourself about what you're feeling. Find useful actions to take, like solving practical problems. If you're angry because your family member is depressed and hasn't gotten out of bed all day, is it time to call the doctor? Perhaps try to find computer-based tasks that they can do in bed that still help the family, or give them short, easy chores they can manage if someone is there to talk to them. It can help to make a list and cross things off, so you can see that you're making a real impact. You'll have other emotions, like worry and grief, so be honest with yourself about what you're feeling. Try to find a healthy way of expressing your feelings and doing something about them. Family members can express their emotions to one another in non-accusing ways like "I know it isn't really his fault, but I feel so worried when . . ." It helps to have someone validate you and confirm that your emotions matter.

Though your family member with bipolar disorder may need your help doing things, always make sure it's really necessary. Most people with a mental illness would like to do things for themselves but can't. Once their symptoms improve a bit, encourage them to push the boundaries of what they're capable of. There will be times when someone has to make appointments for them, drive them around, or make sure they eat and take medication. The good news: You can hand these tasks back to the person with bipolar disorder as soon as they can handle things. Expressed emotion, the toxic atmosphere that increases symptoms, includes overinvolvement. Letting them do things for themselves once they feel better is just as important as stepping in when they need you. They need to eat, but it's fine if you let them heat up some leftovers instead of cooking just for them.

One of the hardest things about caring for someone with bipolar is protecting them and the rest of your family from the consequences of their actions. This may not always be possible. Part of mania and hypomania is the inability to see that actions will have negative consequences. Do the best you can and let go of what you can't control. If someone tends to go into debt, take their credit cards and hide them. If your loved one binges on drugs or alcohol, do your best to keep them involved in activities at home with family who won't enable that. If they insist that they're going to become a major beauty influencer by next week, let them take all the selfies they want and maybe have a small budget to buy makeup, but try to prevent them from doing anything that might be damaging to them or the family later.

Do your best not to blame or give orders to someone in a severe mood episode. It won't have any effect: You can't order a symptom not to exist. Blaming someone with an illness doesn't make it go away, and everyone involved will end up more frustrated.

Living Together

Because bipolar disorder often emerges during adolescence and in the early twenties, the person with bipolar disorder will likely be living with relatives or roommates when the first mood episode occurs. One of the first things to consider after your loved one receives a diagnosis is how much support they need. Can family or friends give the person what they need right now? If the person seems to have milder moods like hypomania or mild depression, that may be possible. If family or roommates can't handle all their needs, it might be time to consider how to get more support. The day programs discussed in chapter 5 (page 69) would help them learn skills and have somewhere to be during the day. A group home is an option for long-term care. If there's any danger, consider the hospital. An adult family member with bipolar disorder living on their own might need to move back in with family during a mood episode.

These are painful decisions, and it's hard for an adult to admit that it's time to let family take care of them for a while. Remember that bipolar is a medical illness. There's no more shame in that than if someone needs care for a serious physical illness like heart disease or asthma.

Check-in

Get the family together to express their emotions. Let everyone state their feelings in a way that doesn't blame others—but it's fine to ask someone to change how they're doing something:

"I feel angry because I'm having trouble sleeping due to all the noise. Can you please wear headphones when you stay up late playing video games?"

"I feel frustrated because I can't sit down and I can't stop all the thoughts in my head. I'm not trying to cause trouble, and I worry that everyone's mad at me and they just aren't saying so."

Be specific about what actions you need people to take. Be open to making some changes to help someone else out.

Keeping Up a Dialogue

Evan's family members were trying to stay supportive and brave for him, but each of them was experiencing loss and grief because of his disorder. Evan's brother, Tyler, had a rift with some friends after Evan slept with a friend's girlfriend during a manic episode. Evan's sister, Kaycee, had to wear a borrowed gown to the prom and couldn't go in the limousine with her friends because the family spent so much money on Evan's insurance and medication. Evan's parents, Charlotte and Don, shared most of the caretaking and were physically exhausted. Evan felt guilt and shame about how his symptoms affected everyone else. The family hid their pain from one another, except in occasional screaming matches when they couldn't hold it in anymore.

There's still a lot of shame and stigma surrounding mental illness, and that makes communication difficult. You might be tempted to keep things to yourself in order to avoid trouble. Everyone will have a lot of thoughts that seem petty and selfish, but there are genuine needs behind those thoughts. The person with bipolar disorder is not the only family member with emotional needs. In order to support one another, family members will need to overcome their barriers about communicating.

How can you do this? It can help to journal about feelings first, so that you know what you need to say. Think about how to make family members more comfortable during discussions. A formal meeting might be awkward, so is it better to do it in a more relaxed way over coffee? Do you need to play basketball or have a bite to eat first? It can help to combine tough conversations with family bonding moments to help you remember that you're all in this together and everyone matters.

When someone is honest about their feelings in a positive, non-toxic way, show them some appreciation. You can thank them, hug them, ask them questions to help them express their feelings, or pass them a cookie—just send a message that expressing their feelings was okay and you hear what they're saying.

It will be tough sometimes. If someone starts to express their feelings in an unproductive way, or a way that will make things worse, tell them that you want to hear what they have to say but would appreciate hearing it in a less accusatory way. Suggest that they try to restate what they're saying in a solution-focused way. For example:

"You all are lazy and aren't doing anything. You don't care that I'm doing all the work."

A response might be: "Sorry, I didn't know you felt like that. Do you have any ideas on how we can help?"

You can set firm limits. If someone starts to become toxic, you can let them know that you want to hear what they have to say, but not if they're going to say it in a degrading way. You can also decide to walk away from the conversation temporarily and offer to come back when everyone can communicate more calmly. You can say something like, "I don't think this meeting is going well. I'm willing to try again later when we can do this without yelling at one another."

It's also important to take responsibility for your own actions and stop yourself when you're getting out of control. Say something like, "Look, I can't do this right now. I'm going to take a break and talk about this later."

The goal is to create a situation where everyone can be honest about their emotions and feel heard and understood, and then shift to being solution-focused in order to figure out how to make this easier for everyone.

You'll know you're doing well as a family when everyone is able to listen and respond without becoming defensive. You're likely to get and give some positive reactions, like "Yes! Thank you! It's about time someone said that."

You can also support someone by reflecting back what they're saying. Just repeat what they said in different words, and ask if you understand what they're saying. For example, if someone says, "I really wanted that promotion and somebody else got it. I feel like that wouldn't have happened if I had the time to work harder," you can say, "You've lost an important chance at work because you've been spending more time taking care of family. You sound sad, is that it?" People usually won't be mad at you if you guess wrong. They might correct you but will be glad you tried and that you're validating what they said.

10 Tips for Talking to One Another

These tips will help you express your emotions more accurately. You might feel awkward or anxious when talking about your feelings at first, but it will get easier.

1. Describe your emotion: "I'm feeling ... because ..."

2. Tell people what you need: "I need you to ..."

3. When someone else is talking, give them some encouragement with eye contact, paying attention, nodding, or saying an encouraging word or two.

4. Validating someone's emotions means letting them know that you hear them and it's all right for them to feel that way.

5. Be supportive but genuine. Put all of this in words that sound like you, not like a TV therapist.

6. Be willing to respectfully walk away from a conversation that's getting out of control.

7. Make difficult conversations comfortable. Have coffee or snacks, do crafts, or try anything else that combines tough conversations with bonding. Think carefully about whether or not to serve alcohol.

8. Take action where you can. Nothing says love like getting things done.

9. Show appreciation for everyone who has helped out.

10. Plan something fun or calming for afterward, so there's something to look forward to.

Understanding One Another

Melissa had finally found the right medications for her bipolar disorder and was feeling much better. She lived with two roommates, who stuck by her through her mood episodes. But now that she was recovering, they still had a lot of leftover feelings about everything that they had given up to help her. Eventually, they all sat down and the roommates talked about how her bipolar disorder has affected them. Their only goal was to be heard and acknowledged. It was a very difficult conversation, one full of tears, and it was tough for everyone to speak honestly but without unfair blame. It wasn't perfect, and sometimes one of them would walk away for a few minutes and then come back when they were ready. With support, Melissa was able to give her friends the appreciation they needed for their actions during the early days of her illness and empathize with their losses.

Family meetings can get easier with time but they're often difficult at first. Do some journaling or have a practice conversation with a therapist ahead of time so that you know what you want to say. During the meeting, focus on listening to others as much as on expressing yourself. Check with them to make sure that you understand them, and let them know when they said something that meant a lot to you. Bring a craft like knitting or something else to do with your hands if it will help calm your nerves. Explain to everyone that you brought it to help you stay with the conversation, not to ignore it. If you start to get overwhelmed, excuse yourself. You can always pretend that you're just going to the bathroom if you're not ready to be honest about needing a break. It's a process.

Remember that you're moving toward becoming more supportive. It's normal for some parts to be difficult. They're all steps toward bringing your family closer together. When it gets too hard, take a break, do a row of knitting, shoot a few hoops, do a couple minutes of meditation, whatever you need—but come back, re-engage, and focus on supporting one another.

Sometimes You Need to Be a Caregiver

A caregiver is someone who looks after the daily needs of someone with an illness. It's a lifesaving job, but not a glamorous one. With bipolar disorder, a caregiver's role will fluctuate over time, as moods and symptom management change. With cyclothymia or mild bipolar II, not everyone will need a caregiver though they may still need some help. Once someone is stable on medication they may not need a caregiver or they may need one only rarely during an occasional mood episode. Caregiving responsibilities can include helping your family member stay in a routine, driving them to appointments, cooking for them and encouraging them to eat, reminding them to shower, picking up a medication and making sure they take it on time, and managing other important details of daily life.

A caregiver usually has to give up a lot. They may have to miss work, spend less time with friends and family, and even have some sleepless nights when things aren't going well. If that sounds exhausting, well, it is. Ideally, there should be more than one caregiver so that everyone gets a break, but that's not always possible.

Caregiving comes with its own burdens. Rates of depression and anxiety are high in caregivers of people with chronic illness, so it can be a good idea to get some support. Caregiver support groups can be places to vent, learn some tips, and hear from people in the same position. If there's no in-person caregiver group nearby, there are online support groups as well as social media pages and hashtags for caregiver support.

Sometimes You Just Need to Be a Supportive Voice

Early on, it might feel like it will never happen, but sooner or later, most people with bipolar find the right doctor, the right therapist, and the right medication. Once they find the right medication, results can happen pretty quickly and there will be more and more days without drama or chaos. The person with bipolar disorder will be able to sleep through the night more often.

By the time you've experienced a few weeks of stability, people with bipolar disorder have often become more independent. They may be able to do without reminders to eat or take medication. They may be able to go to appointments or pick up medication by themselves.

When this happens, the caregiver's role will start to change. Family members may find themselves hovering over the mood and symptom log looking for the slightest sign of relapse. It will take a while for that anxiety to fade.

This change will come as a relief, but caregivers might have some anxiety as they spend less time taking care of the family member. They will need a while to get used to the calm and transition back to a more normal lifestyle and a different role. The caregiver might eventually transition into the role of a supportive voice. As the person with bipolar becomes more independent they'll need someone to bounce ideas off of and vent to about their anxieties, as well as someone to celebrate accomplishments with.

No matter how stable someone becomes, there will probably be another mood episode eventually. The caregiver should do their best to enjoy the stable times and go back to focusing on their own lives, while they remain emotionally supportive.

Being an Advocate

Mental health advocacy is the next level of support for people with mental illness and their families. Some people want to fight for mental health on a social or political level, and there are a lot of ways to do that with varying levels of commitment:

→ Start a blog or vlog about living with someone with mental illness. Don't share anyone else's private information without their consent. You can do a blog under a pen name for privacy if you want.

→ Contribute to a podcast about mental illness by offering to be a guest speaker or by writing in with a personal story.

→ Donate to or fundraise for a mental health advocacy group.

→ Take part in a walk/run fundraiser for mental health.

→ Learn about the politics of health care and contact politicians about better care for mental illness.

→ Volunteer for a local mental health organization.

→ Write articles or speak about mental illness.

→ Use social media to encourage people to talk about mental illness and reduce stigma.

Before you do any advocacy work, make sure that you talk it over with family. Choose a form of advocacy that won't violate anyone's privacy and make sure that everyone included has consented to it. People still lose friends, relationships, jobs, and housing over stigma toward mental illness, so don't take that chance with anyone else's private experiences.

There are several organizations listed in the Resources section (page 150) in the back of this book. They all offer different options that might help your family, including support groups, psychoeducation groups, or political action committees. And don't worry if you don't have time for advocacy now; you can always get involved later when your family has its needs met. If an organization seems to be asking a lot from you without offering you anything of value, move on to a different organization.

In this chapter we worked on communication and team-building. Chapter 9 will continue the theme of family relationships by focusing on setting boundaries, handling crises, and managing emotions around rifts between family members—as well as why getting some distance can sometimes be better in the long term.

Boundaries and Healthy Relationships

Relationships where everyone has to be perfect are not healthy because everyone has to hide so much of themselves. Healthy relationships include productive arguments, free expression of needs, and space to be alone. In this chapter, we'll look at creating and maintaining healthy relationships through boundaries, conversation, and self-care.

It's Okay to Need Space

Gillian, a high school senior, had bipolar I, while her sister Teresa, a high school sophomore, was neurotypical (no neurological or mental illness). When Gillian was in a manic state, life revolved around her. As the "normal" sister, Teresa was expected to miss parties, dances, and sporting events because of financial and time limits. She often lost study time and sleep because of the chaos during a manic episode. While some of this was inevitable, Teresa was treated as though she was wrong for wanting to have a life despite her sister's bipolar disorder. She was further alienated from her friends because the family expected her to keep their problems a secret. When Teresa spent the night at friends' houses to study and have fun, her parents made her feel guilty. When she wasn't able to study enough at home because helping take care of her sister took up so much time and energy, her parents complained her grades weren't good enough.

Everyone has legitimate needs, not just the person with bipolar disorder. Everyone needs time alone, a social life, and respect for their time and space. In the previous example, Gillian and Teresa's parents are probably also tired and sad about giving up important parts of their own lives. But bipolar disorder is a long-term illness; if family members don't have the time and space to live their own lives outside of others' needs, it can lead to arguments and burnout. It creates ruptures in the family that can take years to heal.

In some families, this kind of stress creates the potential for violence. There need to be strong boundaries in every family so that violence is never acceptable, no matter who the victim or perpetrator is. People with mental illness don't have significantly higher rates of domestic violence than the general population, and people with bipolar disorder are a lot more likely to be the victims of violence than the perpetrators. Substance abuse in the home strongly contributes to domestic abuse.

What Do Boundaries Look Like?

Boundaries are the limits that someone sets on how others are allowed to treat them. Healthy boundaries are the space in which a person can love both themselves and the other person at the same time. Boundaries can be physical, sexual, emotional, verbal, or financial.

People with bipolar disorder are more prone to violating other people's boundaries when they're having manic or hypomanic symptoms because of the grandiose thoughts and low impulse control. Other family members may have to set and maintain boundaries and back one another up.

Financial boundaries are especially complicated because mental illness is expensive. A conversation about financial boundaries might involve making sure everyone has some money to spend, and that family members are protected from the financial consequences of mental illness as much as possible.

An overinvolved caregiver might need to set boundaries with themselves. Instead of cooking three times a day for someone who isn't eating enough, consider batch-cooking, breakfast/snack bars, shakes, or other prepared meals. Instead of watching the person with bipolar constantly, it might be safe to only look in on them once in a while.

There will be arguments sometimes. That's the reality of being part of any family. A healthy argument must have the following boundaries:

→ Step back and give everyone a few minutes to calm down if they need to. Don't insist on having an argument while tempers are flaring.
→ Keep the argument solution-focused. What happened that caused a problem? What are the possible ways to deal with it? Which one works for the most people?
→ Talking about blame never helps. If the conversation shifts to blame, shift it to possible solutions.

→ Everyone should keep their body language non-defensive and non-threatening. Nobody should be towering over anyone or sitting in a way that implies rejection. Body language should imply that everyone is listening.

→ Set boundaries with yourself and others. Listen if others communicate problems respectfully, but know that you can leave the situation if anyone shows blaming or aggressive behavior. If this becomes a recurring issue, look into anger management. The Resources section (page 150) has a couple of good workbooks on anger management.

Creating Boundaries

Jim and John were brothers who lived together. John had bipolar II disorder, and Jim was his caregiver. Both were able to work most of the time, although John occasionally took a month-long medical leave due to severe depression. They had to set boundaries about finances. John didn't have good health insurance, so he set aside some money every month for copays and emergencies. Jim learned not to hover over John when it wasn't necessary. When hypomanic, John gave his brother very little personal space or time. Friends often took John out so both brothers could get some peace.

Boundaries should be a win-win situation whenever possible. Everyone might not get everything they want, but they should get enough of what they want.

To start setting boundaries, family members can do the following:

→ Express their most important areas of frustration.

→ Validate one another's needs. Don't treat others like their needs don't matter.

→ Look for the win-win situation. If one family member needs more time at work and another needs more time with friends, how can they have both? Sometimes egos will push people to try to "win" when a compromise would be just as good.

→ Expect some resistance and negotiation. Stay strong about boundaries but be open to creative ideas about how those needs can be met. If someone needs a ride to work, there are probably multiple options for making that happen.

→ Find ways that the person with bipolar disorder can contribute something regardless of their mood episode. Someone with depression might still be able to do household tasks online, or be home for deliveries or hired help. Someone with mania or hypomania could do some batch-cooking or cleaning.

STATEMENTS THAT SET BOUNDARIES

"I've been so busy taking care of things at home that I'm not keeping up at work, and my performance review wasn't that great. I'm going to need some help."

"I don't have any big meetings until afternoon, so I can be available in the morning."

"I'll be okay if I play video games and work on my social media page. I don't know what we need to buy, but if you want to order groceries online, I can be around to receive them and put them away if it's before 3 p.m."

How Involved Do You Want to Be?

Kate's bipolar disorder made life chaotic for her family, and her siblings felt overburdened during her severe mood episodes. Her sister Celia received a scholarship to a college a few hundred miles away and only returned on vacations. She accepted the fact that the family couldn't send her money; when she was home she helped out only when it didn't interrupt school or work. Her brother Cameron moved across town. He contributed money and time, but he also got married and had his own family to care for. Kate worked hard to achieve stability. In time, she could take care of herself and rent her own apartment, so her parents did not have to care for her very much as they got older. Even with her success, it took a while to repair broken bonds.

Every family member will have to decide how much they can be involved. Ideally, multiple family members contribute to care so no one handles everything alone, but that isn't always realistic. Someone who wants minimal involvement might be willing to do something easy, like pick up prescriptions or do some housework. Some people, especially if they've been hurt physically or emotionally, may choose not to be involved at all. It's usually best to respect that for the long-term stability of the family.

When young children are in the house, adults should explain to them that a family member has an illness that can be scary and upsetting, and that everyone is working on finding the right doctors and medicine. The child's opinions should be heard when decisions will affect them, or a lack of information might hurt them. Children don't need all the details, but having a huge mystery in the house can be scarier than a little age-appropriate education about bipolar: "Mommy has an illness in her brain. We're taking her to the doctor for medicine, but it might take her a long time to feel better. She still loves you. It will be easier to see that once she gets better."

Give the child a simple plan to follow in case of emergency, like, "If Mommy gets really angry again, I want you to go to your room and play in there by yourself. That's part of her brain illness. We'll handle it." Someone should sit with a child if possible when things are chaotic, or the child can be taken to a friend or neighbor. But keep the child informed.

Maintaining Healthy Family Relationships

Family relationships should be one of your biggest assets when trying to cope with mental illness in the family. If family relationships are already strained, involve a family therapist as soon as possible, or a spiritual leader if that's part of your family's traditions. Try to find one who's informed about mental illness.

Wherever there are already strong bonds, put effort into keeping them. Keep making time for one another and talking about problems as well as having fun together. In a healthy family, bipolar isn't the only topic of conversation. Shared interests and hobbies are a big strength and give everyone a much-needed feeling of normalcy. Keep up family traditions, even if they need a little modification for the family member with bipolar disorder to feel included. You might have to work more physical activity into Thanksgiving when your loved one is hypomanic, or understand that they might need to sleep through part of a holiday if they're in a depressive episode.

Staying Healthy and Caring for Yourself

Family relationships are based on caring for one another as well as giving everyone a chance to care for themselves. Instagram-worthy levels of self-care aren't always realistic, particularly during the most difficult times. Part of self-care is being realistic about what you can get done. Look out for the family members who are absolutely terrible at remembering self-care. Challenge their belief that they should come last.

Self-care is how you answer the question "What would I be doing right now if I really cared about myself?" Self-care is also balanced against others' needs. Holding that balance, how would you answer that question? We often default to food or alcohol as a way of coping, but your body might need rest, exercise, or a chance to be away from the tension for a while to relax. Your mind might need deep philosophy, but it might also need silliness and humor.

Friends

Talking to friends about bipolar disorder can be intimidating. Mental illness still carries stigma, and talking about it outside the family carries risks as well as benefits. However, treating bipolar as a shameful secret will become toxic in the long term. Bipolar disorder is an illness just like any other and shouldn't be a cause for shame any more than cancer or lupus would be.

If friends express concern for you, let them know whether you want to talk about it or not:

"I usually don't talk much about it, but could I vent for a while?"

"I need to have some fun today. Let's just go out for a while and talk about other things."

> **Check-in**
>
> Get the family together for a few minutes, and make sure everyone has their planners. Schedule in some time for each family member to get away and be with friends or take some time for self-care. Treat this like any other appointment: It's important and essential.

Safety and Crisis

Hopefully you've written out the part of the action plan that spells out what family members will do if they need to manage a psychiatric emergency. If not, do that right away.

It's normal to feel fear, anger, irritation, or even boredom when you have to manage a crisis. Emergency plans help you make thoughtful decisions at times when you're tempted to react out of impulse or emotion.

If the family member with bipolar disorder tends to get violent or agitated, one or two family members (or more) can take a class or read a book on nonviolent crisis intervention or violence de-escalation. If symptoms include suicidal thoughts or urges, there are classes in suicide prevention that advise on how to talk to someone who is suicidal—though if there's any immediate risk, always get them to the hospital.

Mental Health First Aid and Psychological First Aid (PFA) both offer excellent classes on crisis intervention, though PFA focuses more on trauma. Anyone who helps care for the family member with bipolar disorder should know these skills. Links to these websites are in the Resources section (page 150), along with some other supportive organizations.

Another tip: Know the difference between your need to control things and what will actually work. Be careful of the urge to strong-arm the situation. Trying to use authority rarely helps, particularly with mania, and it often makes things worse and damages relationships. Think about what worked in the past. Make use of healthy relationships in the family to help someone manage symptoms. When you can, flow with the situation instead of against it. Use safe physical activity as an outlet for someone with mania or hypomania, or listen to music or have long conversations to help someone with depression manage their feelings.

Financial Issues

One of the most stressful questions about mental illness is how to pay for mental health care. In the United States, the health-care system typically assumes that someone has good insurance. Check your insurance policy to see what services are covered. Call and ask about copays, deductibles, and coinsurance, all of which are costs of care that insurance doesn't cover. Do this for every provider on your treatment team—psychiatrists are often reimbursed very differently than therapists.

If your family member doesn't have insurance, most hospitals and community mental health agencies have staff who will help patients and families through this. Talk to the case manager or social worker about unemployment, disability payments, Medicaid, Medicare, and any other financial help that's available in your state.

If insurance is limited and your family member doesn't need a hospital or community health, finding a therapist who takes "private pay" is another option. Private pay means that you pay cash for therapy. Ask if they have a sliding fee scale, which is when a therapist will lower the cost of a session based on family income and number of family members. To get a sliding fee scale, you'll have to provide some proof of income, like a paycheck stub or tax return. Occasionally, someone's costs with insurance are so high that the therapist's sliding fee scale might be less expensive.

Your therapist will likely require a credit or debit card on file for any cash payment, including copays and deductibles. Another option is either a health spending account or flexible spending account. These are health-related savings accounts that allow people to pay for health-care costs with pre-tax dollars.

Check the insurance policy to see if ambulances are covered in the event they have to go to the hospital. If the ambulance isn't covered, drive them to the hospital as long as it's safe to do so.

Work

Some people with bipolar disorder are on permanent disability and receive social security disability. Others have full-time jobs and families of their own. Many people function anywhere in between those two extremes. Wherever they're at, it's a good idea to have a plan for if bipolar disorder disrupts your family member's income. Most people with bipolar disorder are employed and may be able to take medical leave using the Family and Medical Leave Act (FMLA).

A mental illness is a legal disability, which opens up some options. State disability insurance (SDI) or social security disability insurance (SSDI), depending on the state, is an option if someone can't work. Employees with disabilities also have legal rights protecting their jobs. In the United States, the Equal Employment Opportunity Commission can provide detailed information about the rights and privacy of people with a mental illness.

If someone needs substantial help finding and keeping a job, look for community agencies that offer workshops and supported employment programs. Research the agency on the internet to find out about their local reputation and ask questions about the pay, benefits, and working conditions to make certain that people who work with them are not being exploited. Like any employer, they vary in their dedication to employee well-being.

Someone experiencing a manic episode should probably avoid making major employment decisions. Look for short-term solutions such as FMLA to get them through until they are stable. If they have a new career idea that sounds irrational but they're determined to pursue it, encourage them to do things like research their new career online, make vision boards, journal about it, or do anything that won't cause any harm. Trying to talk someone out of an idea during a manic episode will just frustrate everyone.

Involuntary Treatment

Involuntary treatment is when someone is hospitalized against their will. It's legal when there is a serious risk of harm to themselves or others and they aren't competent to make decisions themselves. The risks of suicide, homicide, or physical violence are the most common reasons for involuntary treatment. Dangerously poor self-care or potentially lethal drug use could also be reasons for involuntary hospitalization. These behaviors may indicate that mental illness has impaired your loved one's decision-making.

Each state or province has its own rules about involuntary hospitalization but there are similarities throughout. On medical units, patients can usually check themselves out if they understand the consequences. Even someone in the middle of a heart attack can leave the hospital if they understand that decision. On a psychiatric unit, it's assumed that people don't have the ability to understand the consequences of their actions when they're admitted, so most units don't allow patients to check themselves out against medical advice.

In addition to being unable to leave without a doctor's order, people on a psychiatric unit can be medicated against their will if they're a danger to themselves or others. If they're not a safety risk, they have the right to refuse medication.

Staff on psychiatric units are trained in violence de-escalation. If a threat of violence can't be controlled any other way, it may be legal for patients to be put in seclusion (locked in a room by them-selves) or restraints (strapped down on a bed until they are no longer a threat). Each state has different regulations about how long this can go on and how well someone has to be supervised for their own safety while in seclusion or restraints.

Family members don't usually have contact with someone in seclusion or restraints. However, checking in by calling, visiting, and making sure that the patient has signed a release of information so family can talk to them will all help protect the loved one from being unsupervised, left in seclusion or restraints too long, or harmed by anyone. Unfortunately, hospital abuse does happen. Frequent contact with family and friends reduces a patient's vulnerability to that.

Difficult Decisions

Luke had bipolar I and came from a toxic family. He had no contact with them because of a history of abuse. He was able to live in an apartment with a roommate and support himself. When he was stable, he was a friendly, responsible roommate, but during manic episodes, he threw wild parties. They often ended with the apartment trashed and the police being called because of noise and drug use in the parking lot all night. At the end of the lease, his roommate moved out and stopped speaking to him. None of their friends would live with Luke. He ended up moving to a cheaper apartment in a dangerous part of town.

Sometimes a friend or family member has no real choice but to break off ties. Living with someone who has bipolar and isn't stable means loss, stress, and, with a small group of people, a risk of violence.

Maybe it took a while to find the right medication. Maybe the person with bipolar isn't medication-compliant. It's normal for people with bipolar disorder to dream of a life without medications, but it isn't always realistic. Family and friends sometimes suffer consequences in the process of getting stable.

Open communication about everyone's needs and setting consequences can help. It's OK to set limits such as "since we know what happens during your manic episodes, I will only move in with you if you stay on your medications." Part of having a relationship with someone who has bipolar disorder is about setting limits.

Transitions

With medications, the support of friends and family, and a good therapist, most people with bipolar disorder can usually become stable. Weeks will pass without a major problem. They will be euthymic (no mood episodes) for longer and longer, or the symptoms will be too mild to cause serious problems. Some people eventually go years without a mood episode. People who aren't on medication may be functional, but they won't be euthymic for as long as someone who takes medication. For those who don't use medication, stability will mean that their symptoms are there but aren't causing any serious consequences.

Make the most of good days. Go out and take some time to yourself. Do something you haven't had time for lately. When the good days become good weeks and then good months, the family can start re-evaulating everyone's responsibilities. Some responsibilities will end, like checking to make sure someone hasn't gone for a walk by themselves at two in the morning or spent their rent check on toy robots. The person with bipolar disorder can start taking on responsibilities such as taking their medication, filling out mood trackers, and going to appointments by themselves.

It will take time and effort to turn a family into a team to treat this mental illness. If the family has experienced mental illness before, then people may already have skills for coping with it, but they may have some bad habits to unlearn in order to be supportive. Giving each family member the freedom to decide how involved they want to be protects relationships in the long run by reducing the feeling of being trapped. But don't let anyone try to carry the load by themselves if it can be helped.

CHAPTER 10

You're on Your Way Together

This chapter is about how to approach bipolar disorder as a team, however large or small your team is. Even if you're blood relatives, your "family" can also include caring friends, spiritual leaders, and other supportive people in your community. As your team works on helping your family member cope with bipolar disorder, remember that you're limited by the knowledge and solutions available to you right now. If things aren't going well, that doesn't mean it's your fault. People do get better with time.

Have Compassion

Ted was a single father whose son, Paul, had bipolar disorder. Ted came home after work one night and saw clear signs of a manic episode. Paul's speech was rapid, he was restless, and he didn't go to sleep until the early morning. Paul said that he hadn't slept well in days but didn't mention anything because he'd hoped that it was school stress, not a mood episode. Ted left a message for the psychiatrist, who had already left work. Everyone felt tense that night. Ted didn't sleep well because of the stress of not knowing how Paul would be in the morning. They almost left for the emergency room several times, but resisted because it wasn't an emergency. In the morning, they were able to talk to the psychiatrist, who saw Paul that day and made some medication adjustments. He told them that they had done well not to overreact.

The brain works differently under stress. You may feel more aggressive or experience a strong urge to control. You may feel intense anxiety. Your brain will push you toward quick solutions that likely won't work. Your memory is more attuned to threats and filters out more positive information. Take a step back and try to get yourself to a place of compassion. When a family member or friend is making things difficult, you can set boundaries with them, but at the same time you can remember everything that's good about them. The person with bipolar disorder does not want to be this way, and they're suffering. Be understanding even while you set boundaries and solve problems.

An Ongoing Process

Kirsten knew that her children were having a difficult time because of her bipolar I. She felt bad, unworthy, embarrassing, and like she couldn't do anything right. She did everything she could to get better, and eventually she became more stable. She had occasional relapses because she didn't feel that she deserved a better life when her disorder caused others so much pain. Finding a medication to control her moods didn't take that long, but repairing her relationships with her children took a while. The hardest part was accepting that she was sick, not bad, and that she deserved to recover.

Things won't always be so difficult. If the family, including the person with bipolar disorder, keeps moving forward, then you will achieve stability. The right medication and the right therapy, plus working on family relationships and finding community and online resources, will get everyone to a better place. The process won't be a steady upward climb. Repeated mood episodes are part of bipolar disorder: expect setbacks. It's not a disorder that anyone truly gets over, at least not yet. It's always possible that there will be a cure later, but for now it's about management.

Progress is limited by knowledge. Right now, the knowledge exists to help people achieve a fairly normal life, but there are still a lot of unknowns about bipolar, such as the exact contributions of genetics, the exact mechanisms by which a first mood episode happens, and, of course, what it will take to create a cure. When setbacks occur, they aren't always tied to something your family did; we need more and better research to understand the exact nature of the disorder.

With so many unknowns, don't hold yourselves to impossibly high standards or expect results that aren't fully under your control. When you look at your own efforts, judge yourself not by results, but by having taken the right steps and done the right things as often as you could. Look for the slow climb. Sometimes things will go backward, and you will be able to handle it.

Some people with bipolar choose to have it treated so that they can move on with life as soon as possible. Their goal will be to live as if they didn't have bipolar disorder. People who know them at work may never suspect that they have a mental health issue.

Others will choose the advocacy route. They may become bloggers, mental health influencers, researchers, teachers, or therapists. They'll be under pressure to keep themselves healthy enough to keep doing that work. Some will choose to publicize their setbacks so that others can see what they really look like and know that they aren't alone.

There's no wrong answer about what route to take. It's a totally individual decision. The important thing is that your loved one feels good as often as possible and prepares ahead for any challenges. Even when they feel good, they'll need to respect their treatment regimen.

In the future, there will be new treatments or even possible cures. Be very careful. Mental health goes through trends like anything else. Just because a treatment is in all the magazines doesn't mean it's been shown to work. Feel free to sit back and wait for the research to come in. It might be a good idea to take a class or read a book on critical thinking and learn how to read scientific research, so you can avoid trends that won't work.

Navigating the Road Ahead Together

Pete, a teenage boy with bipolar II, lived with a family that was not supportive of him. They loved him, but when he had a mood episode, they took a disciplinary approach to it. He felt like a failure when he couldn't do what they wanted, like calm down and stop getting so excited about things. One night, when his hypomania was keeping him awake, he got in touch with some people online who had bipolar disorder. Those conversations led him to the mental health advocacy community. Everyone on the bipolar message board he found was talking about experiences just like his. It was terrifying to think that he had a mental health disorder, but these people were also pointing out that it wasn't their fault and they weren't bad people. There were bullies and trolls online, which was hard, but there were also people standing up to them and educating others about bipolar disorder. This "found family" got him through until he was old enough to seek treatment on his own.

It's easy to envision everything that could have gone wrong in this story. Based on the information in this book and other sources, how could Pete's family have better handled the situation? What risks did Pete take by getting his emotional support from strangers on the Internet?

Some people with bipolar disorder can't get support from their family. People who are rejected at home find supportive "found families" online, in fandoms, in religious groups, among people with shared intellectual interests, and in other places; but there's no substitute for a supportive family around you. Forcing someone to find emotional support elsewhere puts them at risk of ending up in dangerous situations.

Family members have lives of their own and can't always let everything revolve around the person with bipolar disorder. They shouldn't try. But give what you can. If all you can offer is emotional support free of judgment, that's more than a lot of people with a mental health disorder have. In this book we talked about expressed emotion and how an unsupportive atmosphere can make it harder to recover from bipolar disorder. Family members should, at the very least, acknowledge that it's an illness beyond the control of the person suffering from it, and that they aren't doing these things because they're bad.

Slip-Ups and Setbacks

A lot of the material in this book is about best practices and the best possible care, so it's an ideal. The goal of the book is to give families tools and ideas that will get them as functional as possible. Nobody is perfect at living up to that ideal, so be forgiving of yourself and others when there are problems and setbacks.

Some of the setbacks will be your family member's mistake. They forgot to run an errand or go to an appointment. They decided to try life without medication without planning for what to do if that didn't work.

Some of the mistakes will be your own, so treat others' mistakes the way you want your own to be treated. At some point, you're going to forget something or lose your temper. You might let something slide because you weren't taking care of yourself or didn't set your boundaries. It happens.

Some setbacks are systemic, like a lack of quality mental health care in rural areas or lower-income neighborhoods, or the challenge of finding affordable insurance with good mental health coverage.

Even if there's no human error, sometimes bipolar disorder is just going to be bipolar disorder. It doesn't mean that anybody did anything wrong. A new mood episode is likely to happen at some point, even if you do an outstanding job at everything within your control.

Keep Going

Bipolar disorder takes up a huge amount of time, energy, and emotion. But bipolar disorder is not the only important thing going on in your family. Love, affection, traditions, and family gatherings are equally real and equally important. Don't forget to celebrate milestones and spend time together for no reason at all. Take your lives back every chance you get.

Resources

Mental Health Advocacy Organizations

National Alliance on Mental Illness (NAMI.org): Run by and for people with mental illness, NAMI works to promote equality and inclusion for people with mental illness. They have chapters in 48 states and oversee educational programs, fundraisers, and events to promote awareness of the needs and contributions of people with mental illness. They have a help line to provide information and support at 1-800-950-NAMI.

Depression and Bipolar Support Alliance (DBSAlliance.org): This organization offers peer-based support, education, and resources for people with mood disorders. They train peer support specialists and work to reduce stigma. If someone is having thoughts of suicide, contact their crisis line at 1-800-273-TALK, or text "DBSA" to 741-741.

Mental Health First Aid (MentalHealthFirstAid.org): A suicide prevention organization that started in Australia but is now worldwide. Among other offerings, they teach free classes on how to manage mental health crises and, for a fee, train people in how to teach those classes.

Psychological First Aid (Who.int/mental_health/publications /guide_field_workers/en/): PFA is an evidence-based and culturally aware program for learning how to help people in the aftermath of a traumatic event.

Movember (US.Movember.com/about/mental-health): One of this international men's health organization's missions is to make it easier for men to talk about mental health and promote early recognition and intervention.

Apps

Wellness: Mood Meds & Health: A place to track mood, medication, and general health. You can even track your history of dosage and how consistently someone is taking their medication.

eMoods Bipolar Tracker: Another mood tracking app. This one doesn't have a way to track medication, but it does track sleep, energy, and other symptoms with charts to show trends.

MyTherapy: A medication reminder app with an alarm for taking medication and completing other wellness tasks on time, a calendar to track history of taking medications, and an inventory manager that reminds you to refill medications when there are a certain number of pills left.

Suicide Safety Plan: This app contains resources for coping with suicidal thoughts, including personal warning signs, favorite coping strategies, reasons to live, contacts, and other resources to help someone in the moment.

Books

An Unquiet Mind: A Memoir of Moods and Madness, by Kay Redfield Jamison: Dr. Jamison is a clinical psychologist who has bipolar disorder. This book is the story of the onset of her illness.

Wishful Drinking, by Carrie Fisher: The actress who played Princess Leia in *Star Wars* was diagnosed with bipolar and addictions. This book talks frankly about her life, including her mental illnesses and time in mental institutions.

The Bipolar Disorder Survival Guide: What You and Your Family Need to Know, by David Miklowitz: A good basic workbook for people with bipolar disorder.

Mad Like Me: Travels in Bipolar Country, by Merryl Hammond: The author has a PhD in public health and was diagnosed with bipolar disorder in her fifties. In telling her story, she focuses on how to help people with bipolar disorder and their families reclaim their lives from mental illness.

Anger Management Workbook for Men: Take Control of Your Anger and Master Your Emotions, by Aaron Karmin: A useful and non-judgmental book. While it focuses on men, it has a lot of good general information on anger management.

Disarm Daily Conflict: Your Life Depends on It, by Chris Roberts: Another excellent anger management book.

Blogs

bp Magazine (bpHope.com/blog): bpHope is an online community for people with bipolar disorder. The blog focuses on the everyday experiences of people with bipolar disorder as well as giving tips about how to cope.

Time to Change (Time-to-Change.org.uk/category/blog/bipolar): Time to Change is another site that focuses on the experiences of people with mental illness. They have a number of writers who regularly blog about their lives with bipolar disorder.

International Bipolar Foundation: (IBPF.org/learn/resources /blog): Another multiple-author blog by people who are living with bipolar disorder, on the website of an organization providing support, education, and advocacy.

Podcasts

Bi-Polar Girl: A couple interviews a variety of experts, including professionals and people with lived experience of bipolar disorder.

The Mental Health Marriage: A podcast that provides support to the spouses of people with mental illness. Episodes focus on learning about and coping with mental illness as well as looking at common relationship problems through the lens of mental illness.

The Bipolar Family: Episodes usually focus on a specific problem, like anger or handling appointments, from the point of view of the family.

References

Aas, Monica, Chantal Henry, Ole A. Andreassen, Frank Bellivier, Ingrid Melle, and Bruno Etain. 2016. "The Role of Childhood Trauma in Bipolar Disorders." *International Journal of Bipolar Disorders* 4, no. 2 (December). doi: 10.1186/s40345-015-0042-0.

Alloy, Lauren B., Robin Nusslock, and Elaine M. Boland. 2015. "The Development and Course of Bipolar Spectrum Disorders: An Integrated Reward and Circadian Rhythm Dysregulation Model." *Annual Review of Clinical Psychology* 11 (January): 213–50. doi: 10.1146/annurev-clinpsy-032814-112902.

Altamura, A. Carlo, Massimiliano Buoli, Alice Caldiroli, Lea Caron, Claudia Cumerlato Melter, Cristina Dobrea, Michela Cigliobianco, and Francesco Zanelli Quarantini. 2015. "Misdiagnosis, Duration of Untreated Illness (DUI) and Outcome in Bipolar Patients with Psychotic Symptoms: A Naturalistic Study." *Journal of Affective Disorders* 182 (August): 70–5. doi: 10.1016/j.jad.2015.04.024.

American Psychiatric Association. 2013. *Diagnostic and Statistical Manual of Mental Disorders*, 5th ed. Arlington, VA: American Psychiatric Publishing.

Apfelbaum, Sergio, Pilar Regalado, Laura Herman, Julia Teitelbaum, and Pablo Gagliesi. 2013. "Comorbidity between Bipolar Disorder and Cluster B Personality Disorders as Indicator of Affective Dysregulation and Clinical Severity." *Actas Españolas de Psiquiatría*, 41, no. 5 (Sept.–Oct.): 269–78.

Bassirnia, Anahita, Jessica Briggs, Irina Kopeykina, Amy Mednick, Zimri Yaseen, and Igor Galynker. 2015. "Relationship between Personality Traits and Perceived Internalized Stigma in Bipolar Patients and Their Treatment Partners." *Psychiatry Research* 230, no. 2 (December): 436–40. doi: 10.1016/j.psychres.2015.09.033.

Bauer, Isabelle E., Juan F. Gálvez, Jane E. Hamilton, Vicent Balanzá-Martínez, Giovana B. Zunta-Soares, Jair C. Soares, and Thomas D. Meyer. 2016. "Lifestyle Interventions Targeting Dietary Habits and Exercise in Bipolar Disorder: A Systematic Review." *Journal of Psychiatric Research* 74 (March): 1–7. doi: 10.1016/j.jpsychires.2015.12.006.

Bauer, Michael, Tasha Glenn, Martin Alda, Ole A. Andreassen, Elias Angelopoulos, Raffaella Ardau, Christopher Baethge, et al. 2015. "Influence of Light Exposure During Early Life on the Age of Onset of Bipolar Disorder." *Journal of Psychiatric Research* 64 (May): 1–8. doi: 10.1016/j.jpsychires.2015.03.013.

Bellivier, Frank, Bruno Etain, Alain Malafosse, Chantal Henry, Jean-Pierre Kahn, Orly Elgrabli-Wajsbrot, Stéphane Jamain, et al. 2014. "Age at Onset in Bipolar I Affective Disorder in the USA and Europe." *The World Journal of Biological Psychiatry* 15, no. 5 (July): 369–76. doi: 10.3109/15622975.2011.639801.

Benedetti, Francesco, Roberta Riccaboni, Sara Dallaspezia, Clara Locatelli, Enrico Smeraldi, and Cristina Colombo. 2015. "Effects of CLOCK Gene Variants and Early Stress on Hopelessness and Suicide in Bipolar Depression." *Chronobiology International* 32, no. 8 (September 14): 1156–61. doi.org/10.3109/07420528.2015.1060603.

Beyer, John L., and Martha E. Payne. 2016. "Nutrition and Bipolar Depression." *Psychiatric Clinics*, 39, no. 1 (March): 75–86. doi: 10.1016/j.psc.2015.10.003.

Bobo, William V. 2017. "The Diagnosis and Management of Bipolar I and II Disorders: Clinical Practice Update." *Mayo Clinic Proceedings* 92, 10, (October): 1532–51. doi: 10.1016/j.mayocp.2017.06.022.

Bora, Emre. 2019. "Neuropsychological Functioning and Neuroimaging in Bipolar Disorder: Evidence of Neuroprogression." *Neuroprogression in Psychiatry* (February). doi: 10.1093/med/9780198787143.003.0010.

Brietzke, Elisa, Rodrigo B. Mansur, Mehala Subramaniapillai, Vicent Balanzá-Martínez, Maj Vinberg, Ana González-Pinto, Joshua D. Rosenblat, et al. 2018. "Ketogenic Diet as a Metabolic Therapy for Mood Disorders: Evidence and Developments." *Neuroscience & Biobehavioral Reviews* 94 (November): 11–6. doi: 10.1016 /j.neubiorev.2018.07.020.

Campbell, Iain H., and Harry Campbell. 2019. "Ketosis and Bipolar Disorder: Controlled Analytic Study of Online Reports." *British Journal of Psychiatry open* 5, no. 44 (July): e58. doi: 10.1192/bjo.2019.49.

Charney, Dennis S., Eric J. Nestler, Pamela Sklar, and Joseph D. Buxbaum, eds. 2013. *Charney & Nestler's Neurobiology of Mental Illness*. New York: Oxford University Press.

Chiang, Kai-Jo, Jui-Chen Tsai, Doresses Liu, Chueh-Ho Lin, Huei-Ling Chiu, and Kuei-Ru Chou. 2017. "Efficacy of Cognitive-Behavioral Therapy in Patients with Bipolar Disorder: A Meta-analysis of Randomized Controlled Trials." *PloS one* 12, no. 5 (May 4): e0176849. doi.org/10.1371/journal.pone.0176849.

Chou, Po-Han, Wan-Ju Tseng, Lin-Mei Chen, Chih-Chien Lin, Tsuo-Hung Lan, and Chin-Hong Chan. 2015. "Late Onset Bipolar Disorder: A Case Report and Review of the Literature." *Journal of Clinical Gerontology and Geriatrics* 6, no. 1 (March): 27–9. doi.org/10.1016/j.jcgg.2014.05.002.

Chudal, Roshan, Andre Sourander, Päivi Polo-Kantola, Susanna Hinkka-Yli-Salomäki, Venla Lehti, Dan Sucksdorff, Mika Gissler, and Alan S. Brown. 2014. "Perinatal Factors and the Risk of Bipolar Disorder in Finland." *Journal of Affective Disorders* 155 (February): 75–80. doi: 10.1016/j.jad.2013.10.026.

Crowe, Marie, Ben Beaglehole, and Maree L. Inder. 2016. "Social Rhythm Interventions for Bipolar Disorder: A Systematic Review and Rationale for Practice." *Journal of Psychiatric and Mental Health Nursing* 23, no. 1 (February): 3–11. doi: 10.1111/jpm.12271.

de Codt, Aloise, Pauline Monhonval, Xavier Bongaerts, Ikram Belkacemi, and Juan Martin Tecco. 2016. "Bipolar Disorder and Early Affective Trauma." *Psychiatria Danubina* 28, suppl. 1 (September): 4–8. PMID: 27663796.

Deligiannidis, Kristina M., Nancy Byatt, and Marlene P. Freeman. 2014. "Pharmacotherapy for Mood Disorders in Pregnancy: A Review of Pharmacokinetic Changes and Clinical Recommendations for Therapeutic Drug Monitoring." *Journal of Clinical Psychopharmacology*, 34, no. 2 (April): 244–55. doi: 10.1097 /JCP.0000000000000087.

Dervic, Kanita, Margarita Garcia-Amador, K.S. Sudol, Peter J. Freed, David A. Brent, J. John Mann, Jill M. Harkavy-Friedman, and Maria Oquendo. 2015. "Bipolar I and II Versus Unipolar Depression: Clinical Differences and Impulsivity/Aggression Traits." *European Psychiatry* 30, no. 1 (January): 106–13. doi: 10.1016 /j.eurpsy.2014.06.005.

Dols, Annemiek, Lars Vedel Kessing, Sergio A. Strejilevich, Soham Rej, Shang-Ying Tsai, Ariel G. Gildengers, et al. 2016. "Do Current National and International Guidelines Have Specific Recommendations for Older Adults with Bipolar Disorder? A Brief Report." *International Journal of Geriatric Psychiatry* 31, no. 12 (December): 1295–300. doi: 10.1002/gps.4534.

Eisner, Lori, David Eddie, Rebecca Harley, Michelle Jacobo, Andrew A. Nierenberg, and Thilo Deckersbach. 2017. "Dialectical Behavior Therapy Group Skills Training for Bipolar Disorder." *Behavior Therapy* 48, no. 4 (July): 557–66. doi: 10.1016/j.beth.2016.12.006.

Ellis, Alissa J., Larissa C. Portnoff, David A. Axelson, Robert A. Kowatch, Patricia Walshaw, and David J. Miklowitz. 2014. "Parental Expressed Emotion and Suicidal Ideation in Adolescents with Bipolar Disorder." *Psychiatry Research* 216, no. 2 (May): 213–16. doi: 10.1016/j.psychres.2014.02.013.

Feingold, Daniel, Mark Weiser, Jürgen Rehm, and Shaul Lev-Ran. 2015. "The Association between Cannabis Use and Mood Disorders: A Longitudinal Study." *Journal of Affective Disorders* 172 (February): 211–18. doi: 10.1016/j.jad.2014.10.006.

Firth, Joseph, Brendon Stubbs, Scott B. Teasdale, Philip B. Ward, Nicola Veronese, Nitin Shivappa, James R. Hebert, et al. 2018. "Diet as a Hot Topic in Psychiatry: A Population-Scale Study of Nutritional Intake and Inflammatory Potential in Severe Mental Illness." *World Psychiatry* 17, no. 3 (October): 365–7. doi: 10.1002/wps.20571.

Fountoulakis, Konstantinos N., Heinz Grunze, Eduard Vieta, Allan Young, Lakshmi Yatham, Pierre Blier, Siegfried Kasper, et al. 2017. "The International College of Neuro-Psychopharmacology (CINP) Treatment Guidelines for Bipolar Disorder in Adults (CINP-BD-2017), Part 3: The Clinical Guidelines." *International Journal of Neuropsychopharmacology* 20 no. 2 (February 1): 180–95. doi: 10.1093/ijnp/pyw100.

Frías, Álvaro, Itziar Baltasar, and Boris Birmaher. 2016. "Comorbidity between Bipolar Disorder and Borderline Personality Disorder: Prevalence, Explanatory Theories, and Clinical Impact." *Journal of Affective Disorders* 202 (September 15): 210–9. doi: 10.1016/j.jad.2016.05.048.

Fristad, Mary A., Stephen M. Gavazzi, and Barbara Mackinaw-Koons. 2003. "Family Psychoeducation: An Adjunctive Intervention for Children with Bipolar Disorder." *Biological Psychiatry* 53, no. 11 (June 1): 1000–08. doi: 10.1016/s0006-3223(03)00186-0.

Garno, Jessica L., Joseph F. Goldberg, Paul Michael Ramirez, and Barry A. Ritzler. 2005. "Bipolar Disorder with Comorbid Cluster B Personality Disorder Features: Impact on Suicidality." *The Journal of Clinical Psychiatry* 66, no. 3 (March): 339–45. doi: 10.4088/jcp.v66n0310.

Ghaemi, S. Nassir. 2016. "Bipolar vs. Borderline–Diagnosis Is Prognosis Once Again." *Acta Psychiatrica Scandinavica* 133, no. 3 (March): 171–3. doi: 10.1111/acps.12560.

Gilbert, Kirsten E., and June Gruber. 2014. "Emotion Regulation of Goals in Bipolar Disorder and Major Depression: A Comparison of Rumination and Mindfulness." *Cognitive Therapy and Research* 38, no. 4 (August): 375–88. doi.org/10.1007/s10608-014-9602-3.

Gitlin, Michael. 2016. "Lithium Side Effects and Toxicity: Prevalence and Management Strategies." *International Journal of Bipolar Disorders* 4, no. 1 (December): 1–10. doi: 10.1186 /s40345-016-0068-y.

Goldstein, Benjamin I., Boris Birmaher, Gabrielle A. Carlson, Robert L. Findling, Mary Fristad, Robert A. Kowatch, et al. 2017. "The International Society for Bipolar Disorders Task Force Report on Pediatric Bipolar Disorder: Knowledge to Date and Directions for Future Research." *Bipolar Disorders* 19 no. 7 (November): 524–43. doi: 10.1111/bdi.12556. Epub 2017 Sep 25.

Goldstein, Tina R., Rachael K. Fersch-Podrat, Maribel Rivera, David A. Axelson, John Merranko, Haifeng Yu, et al. 2015. "Dialectical Behavior Therapy for Adolescents with Bipolar Disorder: Results from a Pilot Randomized Trial." *Journal of Child and Adolescent Psychopharmacology* 25, no. 2 (March): 140–9. doi: 10.1089/cap.2013.0145.

Harvey, Allison G., Adriane M. Soehner, Kate A. Kaplan, Kerrie Hein, Jason Lee, Jennifer Kanady, et al. 2015. "Treating Insomnia Improves Mood State, Sleep, and Functioning in Bipolar Disorder: A Pilot Randomized Controlled Trial." *Journal of Consulting and Clinical Psychology* 83, no. 3 (June): 564. doi: 10.1037/a0038655.

Haukvik, Unn Kristin, Thomas F. McNeil, Elisabeth H. Lange, Ingrid Melle, Anders M. Dale, Ole A. Andreassen, and Ingrid Agartz. 2014. "Pre- and Perinatal Hypoxia Associated with Hippocampus/ Amygdala Volume in Bipolar Disorder." *Psychological Medicine* 44, no. 5 (April): 975–85. doi: 10.1017/S0033291713001529.

Hubbard, Alison A., Peter M. McEvoy, Laura Smith, and Robert Thomas Kane. 2016. "Brief Group Psychoeducation for Caregivers of Individuals with Bipolar Disorder: A Randomized Controlled Trial." *Journal of Affective Disorders* 200 (August): 31–6. doi: 10.1016/j.jad.2016.04.013.

Hunt, Glenn E., Gin S. Malhi, Michelle Cleary, Harry Man Xiong
Lai, and Thiagarajan Sitharthan. 2016. "Comorbidity of Bipolar
and Substance Use Disorders in National Surveys of General
Populations, 1990–2015: Systematic Review and Meta-analysis."
Journal of Affective Disorders 206 (December): 321–30.
doi: 10.1016/j.jad.2016.06.051.

Inder, Maree L., Marie T. Crowe, Suzanne E. Luty, Janet D. Carter,
Stephanie Moor, Christopher M. Frampton, and Peter R. Joyce.
2015. "Randomized, Controlled Trial of Interpersonal and Social
Rhythm Therapy for Young People with Bipolar Disorder."
Bipolar Disorders 17, no. 2 (March): 128–38. doi: 10.1111/bdi.12273.

International Bipolar Foundation. "Bipolar Disorder Medications."
Accessed May 18, 2020. IBPF.org/learn/education/treatment
/medications.

Johnson, Lars, Ola Lundström, Anna Åberg-Wistedt, and Aleksander
A. Mathé. 2003. "Social Support in Bipolar Disorder: Its
Relevance to Remission and Relapse." *Bipolar Disorders* 5,
no. 2 (April): 129–37. doi: 10.1034/j.1399-5618.2003.00021.x.

Kim, Eunice, and David J. Miklowitz. 2004. "Expressed Emotion
as a Predictor of Outcome among Bipolar Patients Undergoing
Family Therapy." *Journal of Affective Disorders* 82, no. 3
(November 1): 343–52. doi: 10.1016/j.jad.2004.02.004.

Knapen, Jan, Davy Vancampfort, Yves Moriën, and Yannick
Marchal. 2015. "Exercise Therapy Improves Both Mental and
Physical Health in Patients with Major Depression." *Disability
and Rehabilitation* 37, no. 16: 1490–95. doi: 10.3109/09638288
.2014.972579.

Krane-Gartiser, Karoline, Mette Kvisten Steinan, Knut Langsrud,
Vegard Vestvik, Trond Sand, Ole Bernt Fasmer, et al. 2016. "Mood
and Motor Activity in Euthymic Bipolar Disorder with Sleep
Disturbance." *Journal of Affective Disorders* 202 (September):
23–31. doi.org/10.1016/j.jad.2016.05.012.

Kvitland, Levi Roestad, Ingrid Melle, Sofie Ragnhild Aminoff, Christine Demmo, Trine Vik Lagerberg, Ole Andreas Andreassen, and Petter Andreas Ringen. 2015. "Continued Cannabis Use at One Year Follow Up Is Associated with Elevated Mood and Lower Global Functioning in Bipolar I Disorder." *BMC Psychiatry* 15, no. 1 (February 5): 11. doi: 10.1186/s12888-015-0389-x.

Lagerberg, Trine Vik, Levi Røstad Kvitland, Sofie R. Aminoff, Monica Aas, Petter Andreas Ringen, Ole Andreas Andreassen, and Ingrid Melle. 2014. "Indications of a Dose–Response Relationship between Cannabis Use and Age at Onset in Bipolar Disorder." *Psychiatry Research* 215, no. 1 (January 30): 101–104. doi: 10.1016/j.psychres.2013.10.029.

Lam, Dominic H., Paul McCrone, Kim Wright, and Natalie Kerr. 2005. "Cost-Effectiveness of Relapse-Prevention Cognitive Therapy for Bipolar Disorder: 30-month Study." *The British Journal of Psychiatry* 186, no. 6 (June): 500–6. doi: 10.1192/bjp.186.6.500.

Latalova, Klara, Jan Prasko, Dana Kamaradova, Zuzana Sedlackova, and Marie Ociskova. 2013. "Comorbidity Bipolar Disorder and Personality Disorders." *Neuroendocrinology Letters* 34, no. 1 (February): 1–8. PMID: 23524617.

Levenson, Jessica C., Meredith L. Wallace, Barbara P. Anderson, David J. Kupfer, and Ellen Frank. 2015. "Social Rhythm Disrupting Events Increase the Risk of Recurrence among Individuals with Bipolar Disorder." *Bipolar Disorders* 17, no. 8 (December 15): 869–879. doi: 10.1111/bdi.12351.

Lex, Claudia, Eva Bäzner and Thomas D. Meyer. 2017. "Does Stress Play a Significant Role in Bipolar Disorder? A Meta-analysis." *Journal of Affective Disorders* 208 (January 15): 298–308. doi.org/10.1016/j.jad.2016.08.057.

Marangoni, Ciro, Lavinia De Chiara, and Gianni L. Faedda. 2015. "Bipolar Disorder and ADHD: Comorbidity and Diagnostic Distinctions." *Current Psychiatry Reports* 17, no. 8 (August): 604. doi: 10.1007/s11920-015-0604-y.

McDermid, Joanna, Jitender Sareen, Renée El-Gabalawy, Jina Pagura, Rae Spiwak, and Murray W. Enns. 2015. "Co-morbidity of Bipolar Disorder and Borderline Personality Disorder: Findings from the National Epidemiologic Survey on Alcohol and Related Conditions." *Comprehensive Psychiatry* 58 (April): 18–28. doi: 10.1016/j.comppsych.2015.01.004.

Melo, Matias, Elizabeth F. Daher, Saulo Albuquerque, and Veralice Meireles Sales Bruin. 2016. "Exercise in Bipolar Patients: A Systematic Review." *Journal of Affective Disorders* 198 (July 1): 32–8. doi: 10.1016/j.jad.2016.03.004.

Melo, Matias Carvalho Aguiar, Raquel Fernandes Garcia, Vicente Bezerra Linhares Neto, Mariana Brasil Sá, Licia Marah Figueredo de Mesquita, Carolina Freitas Cardeal de Araújo, and Veralice Meireles Sales de Bruin. 2016. "Sleep and Circadian Alterations in People at Risk for Bipolar Disorder: A Systematic Review." *Journal of Psychiatric Research* 83 (December): 211–9. doi: 10.1016/j.jpsychires.2016.09.005.

Messer, Thomas, Gero Lammers, Florian Müller-Siecheneder, Raluca-Florela Schmidt, and Sahar Latifi. 2017. "Substance Abuse in Patients with Bipolar Disorder: A Systematic Review and Meta-analysis." *Psychiatry Research* 253 (July): 338–50. doi: 10.1016/j.psychres.2017.02.067.

Miklowitz, David J., and Bowen Chung. 2016. "Family-Focused Therapy for Bipolar Disorder: Reflections on 30 Years of Research." *Family Process* 55, no. 3 (September): 483–99. doi: 10.1111/famp.12237.

Miklowitz, David J., Michael W. Otto, Ellen Frank, Noreen A. Reilly-Harrington, Jane N. Kogan, Gary S. Sachs, et al. 2007. "Intensive Psychosocial Intervention Enhances Functioning in Patients with Bipolar Depression: Results from a 9-month Randomized Controlled Trial." *American Journal of Psychiatry* 164, no. 9 (September): 1340–7. doi: 10.1176/appi.ajp.2007.07020311.

Miller, Laura J., and Nafisa Y. Ghadiali. 2015. "Gender-specific Mental Health Care Needs of Women Veterans Treated for Psychiatric Disorders in a Veterans Administration Women's Health Clinic." *Medical Care* 53, suppl 1. (April): S93–6. doi: 10.1097/MLR.0000000000000282.

Mondimore, Francis Mark. 2014. *Bipolar Disorder: A Guide for Patients and Families*, 3rd ed. Baltimore, MD: Johns Hopkins University Press.

Mueser, Kim T., Jennifer D. Gottlieb, Corrine Cather, Shirley M. Glynn, Roberto Zarate, Lindy F. Smith. 2012. "Antisocial Personality Disorder in People with Co-occurring Severe Mental Illness and Substance Use Disorders: Clinical, Functional, and Family Relationship Correlates." *Psychosis* 4, no. 1 (January 1): 52–62. doi: 10.1080/17522439.2011.639901.

Nabavi, Behrouz, Alex J. Mitchell, and David Nutt. 2015. "A Lifetime Prevalence of Comorbidity between Bipolar Affective Disorder and Anxiety Disorders: A Meta-analysis of 52 Interview-based Studies of Psychiatric Population." *EBioMedicine* 2, no. 10 (September 8): 1405–19. doi: 10.1016/j.ebiom.2015.09.006.

Narayanaswamy, Janardhanan C., Nagaraj Moily, Shobana Kubendran, Y. C. Janardhan Reddy, and Sanjeev Jain. 2014. "Does Latitude as a Zeitgeber Affect the Course of Bipolar Affective Disorder?" *Medical Hypotheses* 83, no. 3 (September): 387–90. doi: 10.1016/j.mehy.2014.06.017.

Perich, Tania, Jane Ussher, and Chloe Parton. 2017. "'Is It Menopause or Bipolar?': A Qualitative Study of the Experience of Menopause for Women with Bipolar Disorder." *BMC Women's Health* 17, no. 1 (November 16): 110. doi: 10.1186/s12905-017-0467-y.

Perlick, Deborah A., Carlos Jackson, Savannah Grier, Brittney Huntington, A. Aronson, X. Luo, and D.J. Miklowitz. 2018. "Randomized Trial Comparing Caregiver-Only Family-Focused Treatment to Standard Health Education on the 6-month Outcome of Bipolar Disorder." *Bipolar Disorders* 20, no. 7 (November): 622–33. doi: 10.1111/bdi.12621.

Phelps, James. 2017. "A More Nuanced View of Hypomania." *Psychiatric Times*, February 7, 2017. PsychiatricTimes.com /bipolar-disorder/more-nuanced-view-hypomania.

Polo-López, Rocío, Karmele Salaberria, María S. Cruz-Sáez, and Enrique Echeburua. 2016. "Outcome of Cognitive-Behavioral Therapy for Relatives of People with Severe Mental Disorders." *Psicothema* 28, no. 3 (August): 227–34. doi: 10.7334/psicothema2015.172.

Poole, Ria, Daniel Smith, and Sharon Simpson. 2015. "Patients' Perspectives of the Feasibility, Acceptability and Impact of a Group-Based Psychoeducation Programme for Bipolar Disorder: A Qualitative Analysis." *BMC Psychiatry* 15, no. 1 (August 1): 184. doi: 10.1186/s12888-015-0556-0.

Qiu, Frank, Hagop S. Akiskal, John R. Kelsoe, and Tiffany A. Greenwood. 2017. "Factor Analysis of Temperament and Personality Traits in Bipolar Patients: Correlates with Comorbidity and Disorder Severity." *Journal of Affective Disorders* 207 (January 1): 282–90. doi: 10.1016/j.jad.2016.08.031.

Quadrio, Carolyn, and Noa Haas. 2014. "Intensive Psychotherapy with Bipolar Disorder." *Psychosis* 6, no. 4 (November): 327–41. doi: 10.1080/17522439.2014.940552.

Quarantini, Lucas C., Angela Miranda-Scippa, Fabiana Nery-Fernandes, Monica Andrade-Nascimento, Amanda Galvão-de-Almeida, José L. Guimarães, et al. 2010. "The Impact of Comorbid Posttraumatic Stress Disorder on Bipolar Disorder Patients." *Journal of Affective Disorders* 123, no. 1–3 (June): 71–6. doi.org/10.1016/j.jad.2009.08.005.

Raison, Charles L. 2018. "Introduction: The Inflammation Connection." *Psychiatric Times*, April 30, 2018. PsychiatricTimes.com /special-reports/introduction-inflammation-connection.

Reinares, María, Francesc Colom, Adriane R. Rosa, C. Mar Bonnín, Carolina Franco, Brisa Solé, et al. 2009. "The Impact of Staging Bipolar Disorder on Treatment Outcome of Family Psychoeducation." *Journal of Affective Disorders* 123, no. 1–3 (October 23): 81–6. doi: 10.1016/j.jad.2009.09.009.

Reinares, María, Francesc Colom, José Sánchez-Moreno, Carla Torrent, Anabel Martínez-Arán, Mercè Comes, et al. 2008. "Impact of Caregiver Group Psychoeducation on the Course and Outcome of Bipolar Patients in Remission: A Randomized Controlled Trial." *Bipolar Disorders* 10, no. 4 (June): 511–9. doi: 10.1111/j.1399-5618.2008.00588.x.

Sachs, Gary S., Anne Temple Peters, Louisa G. Sylvia, and Heinz Grunze. 2014. "Polypharmacy and Bipolar Disorder: What's Personality Got to Do with It?" *International Journal of Neuropsychopharmacology* 17, no. 7, (July): 1053–61. doi: 10.1017/S1461145713000953.

Salcedo, Stephanie, Alexandra K. Gold, Sana Sheikh, Peter H. Marcus, Andrew A. Nierenberg, Thilo Deckersbach, and Louisa G. Sylvia. 2016. "Empirically Supported Psychosocial Interventions for Bipolar Disorder: Current State of the Research." *Journal of Affective Disorders* 201 (September 1): 203–14. doi: 10.1016/j.jad.2016.05.018.

Sampogna, Gaia, Mario Luciano, Valeria Del Vecchio, Claudio Malangone, Corrado De Rosa, Vincenzo Giallonardo, et al. 2018. "The Effects of Psychoeducational Family Intervention on Coping Strategies of Relatives of Patients with Bipolar I Disorder: Results from a Controlled, Real-World, Multicentric Study." *Neuropsychiatric Disease and Treatment* 14 (April 11): 977–89. doi: 10.2147/NDT.S159277.

Shorter, Edward. 2009. "The History of Lithium Therapy." *Bipolar Disorders* 11, suppl. 1 (June): 4–9. doi: 10.1111/j.1399-5618.2009.00706.x.

Singh, Bhupendra, A.N. Verma, and Amool R. Singh. 2014. "Psychosocial Characteristics of Rehospitalization among Bipolar Affective Disorder Patients." *Indian Journal of Health & Wellbeing* 5, no. 12: 1434–38.

Singh, Tanvir, and Muhammad Rajput. 2006. "Misdiagnosis of Bipolar Disorder." *Psychiatry (Edgmont)* 3, no. 10 (October): 57. PMID: 20877548.

Smilowitz, Stephen, Awais Aftab, Michelle Aebi, Jennifer Levin, Curtis Tatsuoka, and Martha Sajatovic. 2019. "Age-Related Differences in Medication Adherence, Symptoms, and Stigma in Poorly Adherent Adults with Bipolar Disorder." *Journal of Geriatric Psychiatry and Neurology* (September 22): 0891988719874116. doi: 10.1177/0891988719874116.

Soo, See Ann, Zhong Wei Zhang, Sarah Jia'En Khong, Josephine En Wen Low, Vamadevan S. Thambyrajah, Syed Harun Bin Taha Alhabsyi, et al. 2018. "Randomized Controlled Trials of Psycho-education Modalities in the Management of Bipolar Disorder: A Systematic Review." *The Journal of Clinical Psychiatry* 79, no. 3 (May/June): 17r11750. doi: 10.4088/JCP.17r11750.

Souza, Érika, Rodrigo Grassi-Oliveira, Elisa Brietzke, Breno Sanvicente-Vieira, L. Daruy-Filho, and R.A. Moreno. 2014. "Influence of Personality Traits in Coping Skills in Individuals with Bipolar Disorder." *Archives of Clinical Psychiatry (São Paulo)* 41, no. 4 (July/August): 95–100. doi.org/10.1590/0101-60830000000019.

Sparding, Timea, Erik Pålsson, Erik Joas, Stefan Hansen, and Mikael Landén. 2017. "Personality Traits in Bipolar Disorder and Influence on Outcome." *BMC Psychiatry* 17, no. 1 (May 3): 159. doi: 10.1186/s12888-017-1332-0.

Sucksdorff, Dan, Alan S. Brown, Roshan Chudal, Elina Jokiranta-Olkoniemi, Susanna Leivonen, Auli Suominen, et al. 2015. "Parental and Comorbid Epilepsy in Persons with Bipolar Disorder." *Journal of Affective Disorders* 188 (December 1): 107–11. doi: 10.1016/j.jad.2015.08.051.

Suryadevara, Uma, Dawn M. Bruijnzeel, Meena Nuthi, Darin A. Jagnarine, Rajiv Tandon, and Adriaan W. Bruijnzeel. 2017. "Pros and Cons of Medical Cannabis Use by People with Chronic Brain Disorders." *Current Neuropharmacology* 15, no. 6 (August): 800–14. doi: 10.2174/1570159X14666161101095325.

Swartz, Holly A., Paola Rucci, Michael E. Thase, Meredith Wallace, Elisa Carretta, Karen L. Celedonia, and Ellen Frank. 2018. "Psychotherapy Alone and Combined with Medication as Treatments for Bipolar II Depression: A Randomized Controlled Trial." *The Journal of Clinical Psychiatry* 79, no. 2 (March/April): 16m11027. doi: 10.4088/JCP.16m11027.

Swartz, Holly A., and Joshua Swanson. 2014. "Psychotherapy for Bipolar Disorder in Adults: A Review of the Evidence." *Focus* 12, no. 3 (Summer): 251–66. doi: 10.1176/appi.focus.12.3.251.

Thompson, Ashley E., Yvonne Anisimowicz, Baukje Miedema, William Hogg, Walter Wodchis, and F. Kris Aubrey-Bassler. 2016. "The Influence of Gender and Other Patient Characteristics on Health Care–Seeking Behaviour: A QUALICOPC Study." *BMC Family Practice* 17 (March 31): 38. doi: 10.1186/s12875-016-0440-0.

Thomson, Daniel, Alyna Turner, Sue Lauder, Margaret E. Gigler, Lesley Berk, Ajeet B. Singh, et al. 2015. "A Brief Review of Exercise, Bipolar Disorder, and Mechanistic Pathways." *Frontiers in Psychology* 6 (March 4): 147. doi: 10.3389/fpsyg.2015.00147.

Tolliver, Bryan K., and Raymond F. Anton. 2015. "Assessment and Treatment of Mood Disorders in the Context of Substance Abuse." *Dialogues in Clinical Neuroscience* 17, no. 2 (June): 181–90. PMID: 26246792.

Varshney, Mohit, Ananya Mahapatra, Vijay Krishnan, Rishab Gupta, and Koushik Sinha Deb. 2016. "Violence and Mental Illness: What Is the True Story?" *Journal of Epidemiology and Community Health* 70, no. 3 (March): 223–5. doi: 10.1136/jech-2015-205546.

Walshaw, Patricia D., Laszlo Gyulai, Michael Bauer, Mark S. Bauer, Brian Calimlim, Catherine A. Sugar, and Peter C. Whybrow. 2018. "Adjunctive Thyroid Hormone Treatment in Rapid Cycling Bipolar Disorder: A Double-Blind Placebo-Controlled Trial of Levothyroxine (L-T^4) and Triiodothyronine (T^3)." *Bipolar Disorders* 20, no. 7 (June 4): 594–603. doi: 10.1111/bdi.12657.

Watson, Stuart, Peter Gallagher, Dominic Dougall, Richard Porter, Joanna Moncrieff, I. Nicol Ferrier, and A.H. Young. 2014. "Childhood Trauma in Bipolar Disorder." *Australian & New Zealand Journal of Psychiatry* 48, no. 6 (June): 564–70. doi.org/10.1177/0004867413516681.

Weber, Béatrice, Françoise Jermann, Marianne Gex-Fabry, Audrey Nallet, Guido Bondolfi, and J. M. Aubry. 2010. "Mindfulness-Based Cognitive Therapy for Bipolar Disorder: A Feasibility Trial." *European Psychiatry* 25, no. 6 (October): 334–7. doi: 10.1016/j.eurpsy.2010.03.007.

Weiss, Rachel B., Jonathan P. Stange, Elaine M. Boland, Shimrit K. Black, Denise R. LaBelle, Lyn Y. Abramson, and Lauren B. Alloy. 2015. "Kindling of Life Stress in Bipolar Disorder: Comparison of Sensitization and Autonomy Models." *Journal of Abnormal Psychology* 124, no. 1 (February): 4–16. doi: 10.1037/abn0000014.

West, Amy E., Sally M. Weinstein, Amy T. Peters, Andrea C. Katz, David B. Henry, Rick A. Cruz, and Mani N. Pavuluri. 2014. "Child- and Family-Focused Cognitive-Behavioral Therapy for Pediatric Bipolar Disorder: A Randomized Clinical Trial." *Journal of the American Academy of Child & Adolescent Psychiatry* 53, no. 11 (November): 1168–78. doi: 10.1016/j.jaac.2014.08.013.

Wilks, Chelsey R., Helen Valenstein-Mah, Han Tran, Alexandra M. King, Anita Lungu, and Marsha M. Linehan. 2017. "Dialectical Behavior Therapy Skills for Families of Individuals with Behavioral Disorders: Initial Feasibility and Outcomes." *Cognitive and Behavioral Practice* 24, no. 3 (August): 288–95. doi: 10.1016/j.cbpra.2016.06.004.

Williams, J.M.G., Yousra Alatiq, Catherine Crane, T. Barnhofer, M.J.V. Fennell, D.S. Duggan, et al. 2008. "Mindfulness-based Cognitive Therapy (MBCT) in Bipolar Disorder: Preliminary Evaluation of Immediate Effects on Between-Episode Functioning." *Journal of Affective Disorders* 107, no. 1–3 (April): 275–9. doi: 10.1016/j.jad.2007.08.022.

Woods-Giscombe, Cheryl, Millicent Nicolle Robinson, Dana Carathon, Stephanie Devane-Johnson, and Giselle Corbie-Smith. 2016. "Superwoman Schema, Stigma, Spirituality, and Culturally Sensitive Providers: Factors Influencing African American Women's Use of Mental Health Services." *Journal of Best Practices in Health Professions Diversity* 9, no. 1 (Spring): 1124–44. doi:10.2307/26554242.

Yee, Caitlin S., Emily R. Hawken, Ross J. Baldessarini, and Gustavo H. Vázquez. 2019. "Maintenance Pharmacological Treatment of Juvenile Bipolar Disorder: Review and Meta-analyses." *International Journal of Neuropsychopharmacology* 22, no. 8 (August): 531–40. doi: 10.1093/ijnp/pyz034.

Youngstrom, Eric A., L. Eugene Arnold, and Thomas W. Frazier. 2010. "Bipolar and ADHD Comorbidity: Both Artifact and Outgrowth of Shared Mechanisms." *Clinical Psychology: Science and Practice* 17, 4 (December 1): 350–9. PMID: 21278822.

Zhang, Liwen, Hui Ai, Esther M. Opmeer, Jan-Bernard C. Marsman, Lisette van der Meer, Henricus G. Ruhé, et al. 2019. "Distinct Temporal Brain Dynamics in Bipolar Disorder and Schizophrenia during Emotion Regulation." *Psychological Medicine, 50*(3), (February 17): 413–21. doi: 10.1017/s0033291719000217.

Index

Acknowledgments

A book like this takes an entire team beyond the author. I'd like to thank my editors, Samantha Barbaro and Gabrielle Moss, and the entire team, including the professionals involved in acquisitions, editing, design, marketing, and everything else that goes into a book. They did an amazing job of getting this book done during difficult times that we couldn't have foreseen when we first launched the project.